TPS SURPLUS

HISTORY ON THE MARCH

ALLAN NEVINS, *General Consultant*

Leaders in Other Lands

BOSTON

D. C. HEATH AND COMPANY

920
E

AUTHOR
JEANETTE EATON

Educational Consultant

W. LINWOOD CHASE, Professor of Education, Boston University

General Consultant

ALLAN NEVINS, Professor of American History, Columbia University, New York

Illustrated by FRITZ KREDEL

4 - 6

Foreword

LEADERS IN OTHER LANDS is a book that tells about a number of persons who helped make the world a better place in which to live. Each of the persons became a leader. And each became a leader because he knew what he wanted to do to help others and would let nothing stand in his way. They were not all soldiers or kings who fought on battle-fields with guns and swords, but they all were good warriors in fighting for whatever they believed could be done. None of them worked for selfish objects. And none of them knew hatred. Even Jeanne d'Arc, when she had led to victory her French troops against the English, prayed for all wounded soldiers, both French and English. Even when Gandhi led his people to freedom, he would not allow them to use violence. And when the Curies discovered radium, they thought only of its help to all people.

In reading this book we shall do well to note a few facts about these leaders and the work they did. They are all interesting people. Why?

For one thing, they really belong to the whole world and not just to part of it. Some people who read this book might say it is about men and women of different nations. It tells about a German printer named Gutenberg, a Scotch engineer named Watt, an Italian artist named Da Vinci, and a Chinese leader named Sun Yat-sen. But this is not the way to look at these leaders. To be a leader of the highest type, like the persons in this book, a man must not think of himself, nor of his country alone, but of all mankind.

v

Another reason why these people are interesting is this: their vision helped them to overcome terrible hardships and difficulties. Just look at Gutenberg! How could he ever have done what he did without a great dream of spreading knowledge throughout the world? He was always very poor. He borrowed money to try his plan for printing. He struggled along in debt all his life. When he died he was poor and almost friendless. But he had won the thanks of the whole world by showing how to make books cheap enough for all people.

We, as Americans, know that our country has, and has had, its great leaders in all fields of work. But it is wise for us to see that many of the efforts of people of other countries have helped us become a great democratic nation.

Not many of us can be inventors like Gutenberg and Watt, great missionaries like Livingstone, or outstanding scientists like the Curies. But this book shows us that there is a place for helpers and followers as well as leaders. In fact, that is why we believe in democracy. The democratic countries offer the greatest aids to men and women who can dream great dreams and toil for great plans. They give scientists, explorers, artists, and political leaders the best chance to make the world better.

We must not forget that great leaders need people to appreciate their work and to follow their ideas. That is where those of us who are followers, rather than leaders, play an important part in our world's history. It is our duty to recognize leadership that is for the good of all people, and to follow it with strength and purpose.

ALLAN NEVINS

vi

Contents

1

HEROINE
OF FRANCE

JEANNE D'ARC, The Glorious Maid

Introduction. HEROINE OF FRANCE

WAY back in 1400 the king of England planned to capture all of France and to rule it. He had reason to think he might succeed. For in those days the people of France were divided.

Some of the great French dukes claimed the English king as ruler instead of the French king. They sent troops and money to help the English in the war. Other French nobles and people, however, wanted their own king. They tried to defend their country against the enemy.

Wars went on for years and years. The English and their friends won most of the northern part of France, including the city of Paris. Slowly they began to move down into the central part of the country. They won several forts there and then laid siege to the city of Orleans. They captured all the forts around the city. But they could not get beyond the strong walls of the town. The Duke of Orleans was a loyal Frenchman. He was doing all he could to hold the English back. So, of course, it was Orleans that the English wanted most to capture. If they could do so, they were sure they could conquer the whole country.

Those were hard days for loyal Frenchmen. When the old king died in 1422, his son Charles should have been crowned in his place. But Charles was a weak and silly youth who did not wish to be king. He let his uncles rule. All he wanted was to have a good time. This was very sad for France. The country needed a strong leader who would give his people the courage to drive the English out.

Nowhere in France could people live in peace. The wars kept people from trading. Young men were always being made to fight in one army or another. No one was left to guard villages and the land. Robber bands roamed around stealing cattle and sheep from farmers. They even burned houses and barns. Yet no matter how little the people earned, they had to pay heavy taxes. Everyone felt helpless and afraid.

Who would rescue them? Often the poor people would ask one another this question. Then someone would be sure to say, "If only the Maid would come to save France!"

People loved the story of the Maid. It told about a wonderful girl who would help unite all of France under a French king. She would wear armor and lead the troops to victory.

"It is said that heavenly beings will tell her what to do!" whispered one person to another. "The soldiers will follow her. She will get Prince Charles crowned king, and she will drive the English out of France. Then we shall have peace. Then our country will be saved."

Many people laughed at this story. But others prayed every night that the Maid would come. She was the hope of all helpless, frightened people.

JEANNE D'ARC
The Glorious Maid

ONE warm summer day in 1425 the whole village of Domremy seemed sound asleep. Nobody was in the dusty streets of the little French village. The men were busy in the fields and the women were quietly at work in their kitchens.

Suddenly shouts and laughter rang through the street. A group of children ran past the houses till they reached one small cottage. Rushing through the neat garden, they called, "Jeanne! Jeanne d'Arc!"

Within the big kitchen the sound of a spinning wheel stopped suddenly. A tall girl of thirteen came to the door. "Why do you call me?" she asked smiling.

Her big gray eyes, her white teeth, and her dark hair all shone in the bright sunlight.

"There's going to be a fight!" shouted one of the boys. "The lads are crossing the bridge from Domremy to the village across the stream. They are going to fight the boys over there."

"Yes," said a little girl with bright black eyes, "and we'll all cheer for the boys of Domremy, and for France and Prince Charles. Please, Jeanne, come with us right away!"

"You know, Jeanne," said the tallest boy, "those people over there are all for the English. It's a shame. We ought to help our boys win the fight for the sake of Prince Charles. Let us cross the stream quickly and help them."

Jeanne looked across the stream toward the other village and her eyes flashed. "I would like to fight for our poor prince. But what is the use of village boys getting bloody noses? When Charles is crowned king, he'll ride at the head of his troops and drive the English out of France."

"But Jeanne," said the oldest girl in the group, "many who pass through Domremy say that our prince only wants to have a good time. They say we'd be better off under the strong English king."

"Never!" Jeanne's voice rang out. "We must never give up our country. It is ours, and the English do wrong to try to take it."

As she stopped speaking the sound of her father's voice floated up from the meadow far below the garden. "Jeanne! Jeanne!"

"It's my hour for watching the sheep," said Jeanne to the children. "Come back later and tell me about the fight."

With a pat on the head of the smallest boy and a smile for the others, she ran through the garden and the orchard. At the foot of the grassy slope, she found her father waiting for her.

Jacques d'Arc was a tall, sturdy man, trusted by all in Domremy. Handing Jeanne the shepherd's crook, he said, "Mind the sheep well, daughter. In these days when robbers are abroad you must not let the lambs stray."

He looked at her gently for a moment. He was thinking how well she did all her tasks. Often the

8

priest of the village church said that Jeanne was a wise child. Although she had never been to school and could neither read nor write, she understood much about the word of God. Jacques knew that all the children loved her. There was always a song on her lips when she sat spinning.

In the quiet heat of the meadow Jeanne walked slowly behind the grazing sheep. Before long she heard happy shouts. Across the bridge from the next village boys and girls were running. Kerchiefs and caps were waving. The moment they caught sight of Jeanne, they yelled, "We won the fight! We won for Prince Charles!"

Laughing, she waved her crook and called back, "Long live the brave boys of Domremy!"

Hot and tired, the children threw themselves down to rest under a big tree. "Jeanne," called a little boy, "come tell us a story. You can watch your sheep from here."

As she walked toward the group, one of the girls cried, "Tell us about the marvelous Maid who will save France."

THE MESSAGE

Jeanne threw back her head as she talked to her friends. "Our country must be saved! And Prince Charles must be crowned in the great church of Reims. It is good that now he is down in his castle of Chinon. There he is far from the enemy. But soon he must leave his easy life and lead his people to victory."

"Who will make him be a real king?" asked one boy.

"The Maid will come," answered Jeanne in a dreamy tone. "She will show him how to be king."

"How do you know?" asked several voices.

Jeanne did not answer. She began walking slowly toward the orchard. It seemed as if she had forgotten her sheep. The children called to her to come back, but she paid no attention.

Some time later Jacques d'Arc hurried up the slope to his orchard. He almost tripped over his daughter who was kneeling on the ground.

"Jeanne! Jeanne!" he cried in surprise. "Why did you leave the sheep? Do you want robbers to steal them? Have you been asleep?"

Stumbling to her feet, the girl looked around in amazement. "Why, I'm here at home!" she said. Then in a low, anxious tone, she asked, "But where are the glorious ones who talked to me?"

"Dream no more!" said her father. "Go back to your sheep!"

But for once his daughter did not obey. Slowly she walked on toward the house. Her father stared after her. What had happened to make her act so strangely? With a slow shake of his head, he went back to the meadow.

Next day Jeanne did her tasks as usual. In the afternoon she helped her mother bake the long, crusty loaves of bread. Just as she finished, a number of children came to get her. They were going to run races in the meadow.

"No," she said gently, "I'm going to the church now. I have things to think about."

Her playmates were surprised then. But when this happened nearly every day, they gave up asking her to join their games. Sometimes when she came back from the little church, her face would be filled with a strange light. Her mother would ask, "Jeanne, what have you been seeing?" But the girl explained nothing.

Who would understand what had happened? Who would believe her? That day in the orchard Jeanne had had a strange experience. She had seemed to be hearing a voice and to be seeing a form of marvelous brightness. Since then, every few days, heavenly beings came to her. In some way she knew what they were saying, and they made her happy as never before. She thought about them as she churned butter, and minded the sheep, and sewed.

Months went by. Then the heavenly beings told her something almost too strange to be believed. They said that she, Jeanne d'Arc, was the Maid who was to save France.

Little by little they told her what she had to do. She must dress like a man and ride to the castle of Chinon to find Prince Charles. She must ask him to give her armor and troops to fight the enemy. For she, a little country girl, was the only one who could lead the French to victory. She was the only one who could help them drive the English out of France.

Jeanne listened in amazement. At first she could not believe she heard correctly. But every few days the same message came. Then she grew afraid. But the glorious beings comforted her. They made her sure she could follow their commands. With no one could she share this secret. She could only pray, and wonder how the great adventure would begin.

Everyone noticed the change in the lively, laughing girl. "Jeanne, why are you so quiet?" "Jeanne, why won't you tell us stories any more?" Her family and the children of the village tried to tease her out of her dreamy ways. She hardly heard them. For she was wondering how she could get to Chinon to see Prince Charles. And then one day her father sent her to nurse a sick cousin in a distant village.

THE MISSION

Jeanne had never been away from home before. This was her chance! From that distant village she might start somehow on the journey. As she walked down the road, she looked back at Domremy. Would she ever see her home town again?

During that long walk she thought of her poor country. If the English armies around Orleans captured the city, Prince Charles would have no army to defend him. He would have to flee, and France would then be owned by the English. Jeanne was ready to fight and die to keep this from happening. But who would let a girl go into battle?

At her cousin's house, while she was nursing the sick woman, she received new commands from the heavenly beings. She was told to go to a nearby town. There she would find a captain who could send her to Prince Charles, if he wished.

As soon as her cousin was well again, Jeanne started off. And true enough, she found the captain and talked with him.

When the rosy-cheeked girl stood before the warrior, he heard her request in amazement. There she stood in laced bodice and a full skirt, saying that she had been commanded by heaven to save France.

"What!" shouted the captain, "I am supposed to send you to the prince to lead his armies?" He roared loudly with laughter. "Girl, you are mad. Go home and mind the sheep!"

Jeanne smiled at him quietly. "Voices from heaven have spoken, and you must obey even as I do.

I will wait here in this town until you send me to Chinon."

Soon everyone in the town knew of Jeanne's mission. Many believed at once that she was the Maid they had hoped would come. A few laughed at the idea. Others were curious enough to talk to her. Among them were two soldiers who had fought the English in several battles. They declared she spoke the truth.

"Jeanne," they said, "we will go with you to Chinon."

At once they went to the captain. "This Maid has wondrous power," they told him. "If anyone can make Prince Charles fight the English, it is she. France is nearly lost. Send us with her to Chinon. Let us see what she can do!"

Finally the captain agreed. He ordered four other soldiers to go along. Jeanne was given a horse to ride and a page's suit to wear. Her long hair was cut short like a boy's. All the townsfolk gathered around to give her a farewell blessing. Then off she rode with the six soldiers. At last the great and wondrous adventure had begun.

TO PRINCE CHARLES

Hundreds of miles they had to go. When the party halted at the end of the first long day, one of the soldiers sprang off his horse and came to Jeanne. "I'll lift you down from the saddle," said he. "You've never ridden a horse before and you must be tired and stiff."

Indeed, she ached in every bone. But soon she grew used to the saddle. The way led through country ruled by nobles who helped the English. Jeanne's party often rode at night and slept by day to keep from being captured. One moonlight night the leader stopped the others on a high hill. He pointed in the direction where, far away, stood the city of Orleans. Then he said, "The English soldiers are camped there. They are waiting for more troops to help them capture the city."

"Hah!" cried Jeanne. "We'll beat that army before more troops can come!"

Not long after that the party reached a region which was loyal to Prince Charles. There the villagers welcomed Jeanne and believed at once that she was the Maid of the old story. From one person to another news of her coming sped ahead of her, even to the castle of Chinon. When at last Jeanne and her six companions crossed the drawbridge of the great castle, pages and men-at-arms stared at her curiously. They made no sign of welcome.

It made her sad that she was welcomed by no one. A page showed her to a little room and food was brought to her. But she was left all alone for days. When she sent word that she must see Prince Charles, she received no answer. Then one afternoon a page knocked at her door.

"Prince Charles will receive you this evening," he said.

The courtiers laughed when they heard that this strange girl said she was commanded by heavenly beings to save the kingdom. On the evening when she was to be brought to the great hall, they wanted to play a trick on her. They said to Prince Charles, "Let's play a trick to see if those heavenly voices have told Jeanne who is the prince." Prince Charles was pleased with the game. He placed a nobleman in the royal chair. He himself stood with a crowd of men and women in the middle of the hall.

Suddenly the heavy curtains at the door were pulled aside. Jeanne in her page's suit entered and stood looking about. Hundreds of candles threw soft light upon the rich velvets, silks, and laces, and upon the jewels and swords. She had never dreamed of people dressed so beautifully.

Every eye in the room was upon this village girl. Everyone was waiting to see the mistake they were sure she would make. A ripple of laughter went through the room. Then, there was a hush.

Jeanne walked toward the staring courtiers. She did no more than glance at the royal chair where the nobleman sat. Straight to the pale young man in the middle of the hall she went. Kneeling before Charles, she said, "Gentle prince, I am sent by heaven to help you and our country."

All the courtiers gasped in surprise. How could this ignorant girl know who was the real prince?

Charles gently drew her to her feet. "Welcome, Jeanne d'Arc," he said.

That night and for days afterward the prince talked with the girl. Her faith that he could be a strong king touched his heart. But he could not make up his mind to act.

"It's no use to try to fight the strong English armies," he said. "I haven't the money to pay soldiers, buy spears and horses, cannon and powder, bows and arrows, armor and food." He spoke like a cross little boy who did not want to do what his teacher told him he must do.

Jeanne was not discouraged. She began talking to the chief captains and noblemen at Chinon. Many of them thought that she was right. They had been longing to fight for France. Now they started planning how to raise an army. Other courtiers, seeing this girl so full of hope and courage, grew ashamed of the idle life at court. They pleaded with the prince to send an army to help Orleans. Nobles and merchants gave money to hire troops. At last Charles agreed.

PREPARATIONS

The castle and all the neighborhood were in a buzz of excitement. Messengers galloped up and down. Loyal nobles arrived from far and near. Jeanne was full of joy. She took lessons in the art of war.

"Think!" she said gaily to the chief captain. "They are making me a suit of white armor!"

One day she begged the captain to go with her to the stables to see the great black horse which the prince had given her. "Doesn't he look proud and fierce?" she asked. "But he is gentle with me. Look!" She held out a handful of grass, and the big horse whinnied and came to take it gently from her hand.

Finally everything was ready. Troops were camped in the big meadow below the castle. The captains and Jeanne went to bid farewell to Prince Charles. All the courtiers gathered on terraces to wave good-by. And over the drawbridge rode Jeanne in her white armor on the proud black horse. She carried a spear with a banner flying from it. Her faithful captains followed the brave girl across the drawbridge.

As Jeanne came in sight of the soldiers lined up in the meadow, they gave a mighty cheer. "On to Orleans! God bless the Maid!"

A long journey lay ahead. After days of travel they drew near Orleans. Then the captains halted to talk over plans. The town stood on a river which had a fine big bridge across it. This bridge was guarded by a fort. To keep the English from entering the town, the people of Orleans had broken the bridge so that it could not be crossed by anybody. Indeed, all the forts around the city had been captured by the enemy. There was just one gate through which it was safe for people to go in and out of Orleans. The French army camped beside the river, and the captains rode with Jeanne through this one open gate.

It was an April evening in the year 1429 when the girl in white armor entered the city. Everyone in the town rushed to greet her. "Rescue at last!" they cried. "The Maid has come to save us!" Strong men knelt in the dust before her. Women held up their babies for her to kiss. Joy filled every face.

VICTORY AT ORLEANS

Five days later the first battle began. The French army began an attack on the biggest fort. Jeanne rode her fine horse to the edge of the battleground. Then she tied him up in the woods and joined the soldiers on foot. It was a fierce, hard fight. The French were pushed back. As the day wore on it looked as if they would lose.

Late in the afternoon Jeanne ran to the very first line of men with banner flying. "Forward, my children!" she shouted. To see her braving danger and to hear her call gave the soldiers fresh courage. They rushed over the walls. In an hour's time they captured the fort. How the bells of Orleans rang out that night!

The next battle was around the fort at the end of the bridge. It took hours for the French to get across the river and into place for the fight. When the fight started, the English arrows fell as thick as rain upon the brave French. Jeanne was always in the midst of the struggle.

As she leaped on a broken piece of the wall, she gave a cry of pain, "I'm wounded!" An arrow had struck her shoulder and buried its head through her armor. Quickly a few soldiers carried her to a safe place. They took off her armor and jerked out the arrow. She wept and moaned, and the men were frightened. Gently they washed the wound with oil and left her to rest. An hour later the soldiers fighting in the rear saw her striding toward them dressed once more in her gleaming armor. She was pale, but smiling. Loud cheers greeted her.

Jeanne looked around in dismay. Many of the French lay dead. Many were wounded. The troops had not stormed even the outer walls of the fort. Sadly the captains said to the girl, "We must stop the fighting for today. It is better to retreat now."

But Jeanne cried out, "No! No!" and ran to the edge of the ditch. Waving her banner, she commanded, "Charge, soldiers of France! In God's name the enemy is ours!"

Over the outer wall the soldiers rushed. With swords and spears they drove the English back. On they swept to the second line of walls, and the enemy fell before them. Then they reached the inner fort. At that moment a heavy smoke came pouring through the open windows of the fort's high walls. The people of Orleans had floated piles of wood under the bridge near the fort and had set them afire. By good luck the wind blew the smoke away from the French troops, but the English soldiers were choking.

Their powder was almost gone. In despair the English ran out to the drawbridge between the fort and the bridge of Orleans. The great weight of so many men upon the drawbridge all at once broke it down. Many of the men fell into the river and drowned. The rest surrendered. The fort and all the cannon were captured.

By the time Jeanne had mounted her horse again, the soldiers had put out the fire. Some of them also dragged up heavy planks to mend the great bridge of Orleans. In triumph they led the Maid's black horse across the bridge into the town. Bells rang. Bonfires were lighted. The city was wild with happiness. As the captains rode beside Jeanne through excited crowds, they shouted, "It was the Maid who led the charge. She alone won the day!"

Everyone wanted to have a great feast for the wonderful girl. But she slipped away to her room and took off her armor. Her shoulder hurt, but she would not rest until she had prayed for all the brave soldiers who had died that day—English as well as French.

Next morning when the captains rode out, they saw the English army marching off. All the forts stood empty. The long siege was over. Orleans was free!

That day was Sunday, the 8th of May. All day prayers of thanksgiving were said. The people called Jeanne the Maid of Orleans and praised her greatly. Soldiers, captains, and people shouted together, "The victory is hers!"

Next day at a council meeting with the captains, Jeanne said, "Now we must lead Prince Charles to Reims to be crowned!"

While Jeanne had been fighting at Orleans, the prince had gone with his courtiers to the city of Tours. Jeanne and the captains went to that city also. The prince received her with honor and thanked her heartily for the victory. But when she urged him to go at once to Reims, he looked like a scared little boy.

"Reims is so far north," he said. "Many of my enemies are in strong forts along the way."

"Have no fear, gentle prince," replied Jeanne. "Heavenly beings are with you. They say you must be crowned at Reims."

Days of argument followed. The captains pleaded with the prince. Finally it was decided that Jeanne and the captains would lead the army ahead of the prince. As they captured towns and forts, he could come on behind them. Happily Jeanne rode off on her prancing black horse.

At each fort there was a bitter fight. Jeanne never left her soldiers. They loved her, and while she was with them they were never afraid. One by one the forts and walled towns surrendered. And so at last, the prince with his lords and captains, the bishop, and the Maid rode into the old town of Reims. Here, as everywhere, shouts went up for the Maid of Orleans. She bowed, dipped her banner, and smiled.

How wonderful it was, she thought, that everything the heavenly voices had told her had come true! Orleans was freed from the enemy. The way to Reims had been cleared. Now she was leading Charles to be crowned king. A girl from Domremy had done all this because the power of heaven had guided her. Jeanne's heart was full of wonder.

A glorious procession entered the great church of Reims that July day. Crowds filled the church and all the square outside. Light which came through the beautiful stained glass windows fell upon the prince, his nobles, and the Maid as they walked to the altar. Charles took the oath to serve the church and his country. Then the bishop raised the crown above his head and called him Charles VII, King of France. Heralds blew silver trumpets, and all the people shouted the words of great joy, "Noel! Noel!"

TOO WEAK A KING

At Reims a council was held with the king. The captains wanted to follow up their victories. "Sire," they said, "the soldiers long to push the English out of France. Let the Maid lead us on to Paris. We can take that city and then drive the enemy to the coast. Victory will be ours!"

"Aye, gentle Charles," begged Jeanne, "now is the time for us to send the English home where they belong."

The king stooped over to pat his greyhound. "Oh, you are always talking of battles!" he said crossly. It was plain that he wished he were back in the easy life of Chinon.

Days of waiting and talking passed. Finally the king agreed to send the army to storm Paris. "Go, Jeanne, if you like so much to fight!" said he. "I shall not go. No indeed!"

Once more Jeanne led her soldiers into battle. The French won again and again. Even the outer forts of Paris were captured. But many soldiers were killed and wounded. Then the army needed more troops before they could storm Paris.

"If Charles himself would bring fresh troops, the people of Paris would slay the enemies within their gates!" said Jeanne. "They would love a brave and fearless king."

But Charles neither came himself nor sent fresh troops. So the army had to retreat. Jeanne and the captains were sick at heart. Even the black horse stopped his proud prancing.

When she joined King Charles again, Jeanne said: "May I go home to Domremy, sire? Since you plan no great battle, you need me no longer."

"No," said the king, "I need you to conquer my French enemies who still are friends of the English."

He sent her out with small companies to attack the castles of these nobles. She knew that with so few troops she would be in great danger. Yet she would not refuse the king. Her only wish was that she might risk her life in a great, last fight which would conquer the English for good and all.

CAPTURED

One night in camp Jeanne had terrible news from the heavenly beings. They said she would be captured. Her heart nearly failed her then. She knew how the king's enemies hated her. But to her soldiers she gave no sign.

One afternoon she led them deep into country belonging to a powerful French noble. This noble was helping the English. He was the chief foe of King Charles. Jeanne's soldiers met a small company of the enemy and drove hard at them. Just as they had surrounded the company, fresh enemy troops rushed up. Jeanne and her men fought with all their might. But they were overpowered. "Yield, Jeanne!" cried the enemy soldiers, and pulled her from her horse.

"We make thee prisoner!" they shouted, and pinned her arms behind her back. She said no word and held her head high.

At the camp where Jeanne was taken the mighty nobleman himself came to see her. With a smile of triumph he looked down at his famous prisoner. "Well, Jeanne, now what have you to say?"

Her gray eyes looked stormy. "I would I had died in battle! But such was not the will of God."

First she was kept for many weeks at a castle. She prayed that King Charles might buy her freedom from the noble. But he made no move to help her. Instead, it was the English who paid her captor a huge sum, and to them she was handed over. They took her at once to be tried in Rouen, a city in a part of France that was ruled by Englishmen.

The French bishops in Rouen believed that Jeanne d'Arc was a witch. They thought that she was only pretending to have heard heavenly voices. The English captains let a court of the church try her as a witch.

They thought if she could be proved to be a witch, the French people might turn against their king. For how could the people serve a king who owed victories and his crowning to a witch?

THE TRIAL

Jeanne looked sadly around her prison room in Rouen. Its thick walls of stone made it damp and dark. Only one tiny window let in fresh air. At night the jailer chained her to a hard bed. The food which was brought to her was poor. She was so lonely in her dark, cold prison that she was glad when the trial began.

The court room was packed. Curious eyes were fixed on the slender figure in the page's suit standing before the judge. Nearly a hundred scholars, clerks, priests, and bishops were there to help the chief judge in the trial. English captains and dukes were on hand to see that too much mercy was not shown the prisoner.

As the trial went on, the judge told her many times that if she would say she had not been led by heavenly beings she might be forgiven. But this she would not do.

"If you command me to declare that the voices I heard were not from God, then that is impossible!" she cried.

People gasped at her courage. Sometimes she made even her judges laugh by her quick answers. Sometimes a murmur of admiration ran through the court. When she was asked about her life in Domremy, she said gaily, "I'll match myself in sewing or spinning with any woman in France!"

This girl was given no one to counsel her. She was alone among enemies. Once she grew ill from living in the dark prison. But usually she looked strong and brave like the young soldier that she was.

It was perfectly plain to her that she was going to be put to death. If the court of the church did not prove she was a witch, then the English soldiers would kill her as an enemy. One day she was taken to the market place and told that she would be burned there, as all witches had to die by fire. She saw the wood piled up and ready. A crowd of people hooted at her. Then, and only then, did her courage fail.

Seeing her tremble, the judge placed before her a paper. It stated that she knew she had been wicked and had been led, not by heaven, but by evil beings.

"Sign this, Jeanne," urged the judge, "and you will be forgiven. The church will only hold you prisoner, and you will not be burned."

Worn out by weeks of questioning, and suddenly afraid, she bent to the paper and put her mark upon it.

But once in her prison room again, she knew that she had done wrong. All that was on that paper was a lie. Now, for the first time since that day in the orchard, she felt deserted by the heavenly beings. No voice brought her comfort. "I must tell the truth!" she cried out. At once she sent word to the judge that she must take back the sign she had made on that paper.

After that the judge declared Jeanne to be a witch and said that she must be burned at the stake.

On May 30th, 1431, Jeanne d'Arc was taken to the market place of Rouen. Dressed in a long black robe, she was placed on a platform to listen to a sermon. Then she was taken to the stake. Townsfolk and soldiers filled the square.

"May I have a cross to hold?" Jeanne asked.

An English soldier answered, "Here, lass, take this!" He held up a rough cross made of two sticks. She thanked him and thrust it into the neck of her robe.

With arms chained behind her to the stake, she saw the soldiers light the great bonfire at her feet. Soon the flames rushed at her. "Jesus! Jesus!" she cried. Those were her last words.

THE SAINT

Suddenly fear came upon the people. One Englishman cried out, "We are lost. We have burned a saint!"

Soldiers and people wept together. Many knelt in prayer. From Rouen the story of Jeanne's courage and her faith in the heavenly beings spread to all the people of France. Many who had laughed at those who said Jeanne was the wondrous Maid of the old story, now believed it.

In time both King Charles and his people said they would do what Jeanne d'Arc had begged them to do. They gathered a great army, defeated the English in one battle after another, and forced them back to their own country. From that time on France was a nation loyal to the French king.

As soon as peace was made Charles decided he must undo the great wrong which had been done to Jeanne. He owed his kingdom to her, and she had been burned as a witch. Nobody believed now that she had been a witch. Everyone thought she was the most wonderful person who had ever lived in France.

Charles called another court of the church. The judge and court declared that the first trial had been unjust and false. They said that only a girl led by heaven could have saved France. Then once more the girl, adored by the people, was called the glorious Maid of Orleans.

Three hundred years later the church gave her its greatest honor. Jeanne was made a saint. And people who do not belong to that church and who live in other lands also honor this heroine of France. They know she was true and loving and brave. The story of Jeanne d'Arc will live forever. For she gave her life that her people might be free.

Talking Together

1. History is the story of what has happened in the days and years before today. It tells about who (people), and when (dates), and where (places), and why things happened as they did. Read pages 2 and 3 again carefully. Then talk about who, when, where, and why.

2. Tell what kinds of work Jeanne did around home. Which of these kinds would the thirteen-year-old girls you know be doing today?

3. Tell the class what you think these places looked like, that is, what the class could have expected to see if they had visited these places with Jeanne.

   Domremy   Reims   Chinon   Orleans   Rouen

Working Together

Divide the class into four committees. Each committee will do one of the projects below.

1. Make a frieze with several pictures on it. Select your own scenes or use these suggestions: Jeanne at home, Jeanne with Prince Charles, Jeanne leads the army, Prince Charles is crowned, Jeanne in prison.

2. Select several scenes that a committee could make into a short play. Decide what you are going to talk about and do. It will not be necessary to write out the parts.

3. Make a picture dictionary. Choose words which need to be explained and which you can show in pictures. Put each word with its definition and its picture on a separate page. Then arrange the pages in alphabetical order, and put them in covers.

4. Plan an assembly program to be presented to the older grades in your school. Plan to use the work done by other committees and any other ideas you have for telling the story of Jeanne and the days in which she lived. Each part of your program must be interesting if you want people to like it.

To Do by Yourself

1. Here are some words which tell how people spoke or behaved. The numbers show what pages to find them on. Look them up and be ready to act out their meanings before the class.

called (5,10)   gasped (33)
shouted (6, 14, 23, 25, 28)   hooted (34)
yelled (9)   cried (11, 16, 22, 30, 35)

2. Find these expressions. Decide exactly what they mean from the way they are used in the story. Be ready to explain the ones you understand to those in the class who may not understand them.

central part (2)   very first line of men (23)
shepherd's crook (8)   arrows fell thick as rain (23)
distant village (13)   the victory is hers (25)
council meeting (27)   murmur of admiration (33)
walled towns (27)   put her mark upon it (34)

3. Make a list of at least ten words which were new to you, or which you do not see very often in your reading. Arrange them in alphabetical order. Be ready to play a class game in which you will ask others to use some of these words in sentences.

2 FATHER OF PRINTING

The Story of *JOHANN GUTENBERG*

Introduction. FATHER OF PRINTING

LOOK at all the books in your schoolroom. Think of all the books you have at home. Then try to imagine what the world would be like if there were no books or newspapers or magazines.

That is the kind of world it was for most people a long time ago. Only princes, and rich men, and libraries had books. Why? Because, for hundreds of years, they were all copied by hand. Few people owned books and those who did treasured them like jewels.

Most of the writings that were copied in olden times were by the Greeks and the Romans. They wrote plays, poetry, history, and books about science.

In the years when Rome had become the center of the Christian church, people began to read new kinds of books. These were written by the early leaders of Christianity. The Bible was the most important.

The task of copying the Bible was given to the monks. They were a special group in the church. They lived together in a large house with gardens and vineyards all walled in. These places were called monasteries. The patient work of the monks helped the whole world.

Christianity began to spread everywhere. Slowly the people in northern and western Europe became Christians.

For a long time it was the priests who taught the sons of princes and nobles to read and write. Then, as more and more people learned to read, they began to see that books were important. All the books they studied were in Latin. For that was the language of the Romans.

As time went on the people of western Europe changed. They stopped fighting so much. They began to do more farming. They made furniture and beautiful things to wear and use. They built houses and ships. Trade became important and in every country merchants were getting rich. They also began sending their sons to school.

When many people had learned to read and write, more books were needed. The monks could not copy grammars and Bibles fast enough for the number of rich people who could buy them. Therefore men outside the church took up the task. Copying books became a trade, and the men who did that work were called copyists. In time these men joined together in a guild.

In those years all skilled workers had to belong to guilds. There were guilds of weavers and woolworkers, of goldsmiths, and of merchants. Each guild had strict laws. The members taught beginners, who were called apprentices. Not until an apprentice had served a long time and learned the trade thoroughly could he join the guild.

The guild of copyists charged a high price for a book. Only a few hundred books could be turned out each year by all the guilds in Europe. Therefore learning spread very slowly.

No wonder that in several countries inventors began trying to find out how books could be copied swiftly and cheaply.

At last, in Germany, a wonderful thing happened! A German, born about the year 1400, made inventions which brought books to the whole world.

The Story of
JOHANN GUTENBERG

EXPLORING THE CITY

JOHANN Gutenberg was born in the German city of Mainz. It was a busy trading city on the river Rhine. All through his boyhood Johann loved the Rhine. Often, after his lessons at the priest's house, he and his friends would walk to the river.

Every step was fun. The boys carried big sticks to chase away the geese and pigs which wandered everywhere. The streets were narrow and crooked. All of them ended at the great wall around the town. This wall had been built to defend the town against enemies. But the gates stood open till sunset. Past the soldier on guard, the boys raced to the edge of the river. There they watched sailing ships start off toward Holland and the sea.

"What do you suppose that ship carries?" Johann often asked.

"Woolen goods from the weavers," guessed his friend.

"Yes," agreed Johann, "and the fine chains and rings and cups made by our goldsmiths."

But the river was not the only part of the city Johann loved to visit. There were the streets where he could look into busy shops. All the shops where things were made were open to the street. People going by could see everything that went on. Johann never tired of watching the workmen. One day he would go home from school by way of the paper-mill where pulp was soaking in big tubs. He loved to see how the soft wet mass was drained and dried and pressed into a sheet of paper.

Another day he would visit a forge. There he would watch a man hammer hot iron into tools, door hinges, and long bars.

Just by watching and asking questions Johann learned a great deal about how things were made. But he was not trained to use his hands.

44

THE SON OF A NOBLE

Johann was the son of a noble, and the nobles did not work with their hands. They thought they were too grand for that sort of work. In fact, there were many differences between the nobles and the common people. None but the nobles were allowed to build houses with more than one story. And they were the people who had the largest gardens and vineyards and orchards.

The nobles were the ones who governed the city under the bishop of the church. But they were a small group compared to the number of merchants and workers. These people of Mainz, who were not nobles, were always unhappy because they had nothing to say about their government.

Johann Gutenberg's father was one of the leaders in the city government. He would say proudly to his son, "Johann, some day you also will take your rightful place as one of the rulers of Mainz."

But the boy had begun to have other dreams for himself. When he was about thirteen years old he stopped one afternoon in front of a goldsmith's shop. Several men were tapping rings and sheets of gold with little hammers. Boys were handing them tools and running errands.

One youth held up a heavy chain to show the master of the shop. The master looked at it carefully. "Well

45

done, lad!" said he. "Soon you can make a jeweled necklace."

Grinning with pleasure, the youth turned. He saw Johann looking in a window of the shop. Johann was dressed in the fashion of young nobles. He wore striped stockings, a fine cloth tunic, and a shoulder cape trimmed with fur. With a sniff, the apprentice spread out the golden chain. It was as if he said, "Don't you wish you could make that?"

Johann was wishing that very thing. He thought it must be exciting to work with gold and silver and copper. Of course, he was glad to be learning Latin. But why could he not be taught to make beautiful

things with his hands also? His wish grew so large in his heart that he forgot the guild's rule that no noble could learn a trade.

Before he could stop himself, he cried out, "I'd like to learn to make a fine gold chain!"

"You!" shouted the apprentice with a scornful laugh. "Why, you're a rich noble's son." Doubling up his fist as if for a blow, he cried, "Go on back to your Latin books, young sir! Leave useful work to common folk!"

A firm hand was laid on the shoulder of the apprentice. The master goldsmith said sternly, "Peace! What harm is there if a young nobleman wants to do

a bit of work with his hands? I know this boy's father
—a leader in our city." With a smile he said to Johann,
"Sir, if you wish, come here every day after school.
I will give you a bench beside us, and you can learn a
little about our work."

Eagerly the boy thanked the goldsmith and went **on**
his way.

LEARNING NEW THINGS

The very next afternoon Johann went to the shop.
The master gave him tools and metal, and told him to
see what he could do.

After that, Johann spent a great deal of time at the
goldsmith's shop. He learned how to cut hard metals

with a sharp tool and how to stamp a pattern into a soft piece of silver. What he liked best was to melt together two or three different metals and make a new metal of them. Then he would hammer or heat it to see how it would behave. He also liked to pour hot metal into a mold. When the metal cooled, it took whatever shape the mold had.

After a while Johann felt he must find out about working with wood. At a carpenter's shop he learned a great deal. Next, a wood carver taught him how to carve things from a block of walnut or oak.

One day he rushed home from the wood carver's shop in great excitement. He found his father sitting by the fire and cried, "Father, I saw a wonderful thing today! It was a copy of the Lord's Prayer on a piece of paper. It was not written by hand. It was stamped on the paper from a block of wood, a block carved with letters."

"Well," said his father with a yawn, "we have seen pictures made that way and playing-cards, too."

"Of course," said Johann eagerly, "but I've never seen a whole page of print before. First the letters are carved in wood. Then the raised places are covered with ink. When paper is pressed down on the block a whole page is printed!"

Johann's father stared at him. "How do you know so much about such work?"

The boy's mother had come into the room. She quickly answered the question. "Our son spends much time in the shops of Mainz. He seems to forget that he is a noble, and likes to work with his hands."

"But I work with my head, too, Mother!" Johann said. "Father Schwartz just told you that I write Latin well."

Johann's parents warned him against spending time with workmen. They said the guilds were unfriendly to the nobles. But the youth could not stop trying to learn new things. He was very proud to find that at the iron-master's shop he could make a shoe for his beautiful big horse.

BEGINNING
OF THE GREAT WORK

As Johann grew tall and strong, he looked much like the other young nobles in Mainz. But they could seldom persuade him to go with them to hunt animals in the forest or to make merry at a feast.

"I'm learning secrets," he would explain with a laugh. "I haven't time for hunting animals."

In his room at home Johann was carving letters on wood-blocks. He wanted to print a Latin poem to show Father Schwartz. The first time he covered the block with ink and made a print of the poem, his heart sank. He had made two mistakes in the Latin words and spoiled the whole block. There was no way of correcting the mistakes. It would take weeks to carve the poem over again.

While he was at this work his father brought him a present. It was a beautiful wood-print. At the top of the page was an angel. Then followed some verses from the Bible.

Thanking his father, Johann said, "This is a fine piece of work. It must have taken ever so long. Think how many years it would take to carve out the New Testament. Men must find some easier way to print a book."

"My son," his father said sharply, "it is time you stopped thinking about such things and faced your duty as a noble. We must all join hands against the guilds. They are trying to take over our government."

Although Johann was shocked to hear this, he did not know there was real danger.

In 1420, the storm broke. Workers and the guild members seized arms and marched against the town hall. All the nobles had to flee from the city.

The Gutenbergs took passage on a boat sailing up to Strasbourg. In that city they settled down. Their power, wealth, and home were gone. Now Johann's parents could not complain because he was a skilled workman. He set up a little shop where he made fine tools and mirrors.

In Johann's spare moments he went on dreaming of a fast way of printing. Sometimes he talked about this with a certain merchant. The merchant sold books which the monks had copied. Johann had often looked at such books in the houses of rich friends and at church. He admired the even lettering and the pictures which were colored so beautifully on the pages. He liked the handsome large letters at the head of every chapter.

"If there were only some way to print books like these," he would sigh.

"Do you know, sir," said the merchant one day, "that certain men are trying to print with separately carved letters that can be moved about? If they succeed, they'll have something better than wood-block printing. For then they will be able to correct a mistake just by changing separate letters."

Young Gutenberg was thrilled with this news. Whenever he had time he worked at making movable letters or type. First he carved letters in wood. But the letters broke easily, and ink sank into the wood and blotted the paper. Next he tried to use letters of lead. They would not take ink the right way and broke when paper was pressed hard upon them. Iron letters were hard to make and they cut into the paper. Johann knew he had to find just the right metal for type.

THE PARTNERSHIP

In 1453 Johann's mother died and left him money which she had managed to save. He rented a house outside the city of Strasbourg. It was near a monastery. The monks living there let Johann use a corner of their big workshop. By this time he had made a great decision. He planned to spend all his time in finding a better way to print books.

For his experiments he needed more money than he had. He asked three men to be his partners in the plan. Each had money to put into the business. They looked up to Gutenberg because he was a noble and because they believed he might make a wonderful invention. Johann made them promise they would never tell anyone about the plan.

One night he invited his three partners to dinner. They brought fruit and wine. Johann's servant served the meal on the long table in the workshop.

"When will this printing business start?" asked one man whose name was Andrew. "My wife is already asking what I have done with the money I had saved."

"And my wife," said another partner, "wonders why we work in secret. She says people think we are magicians."

Gutenberg had heard this before. "Let us not be worried by what others think," he cried. "But I must tell you, friends, that this work will take time. It cannot be done in haste."

Then and there he gave his partners a list of all the things he had to do. First he had to find the right metal to mold type. Next, he had to make the molds and a tool called a punch which stamped the shape of a letter into the mold. A separate punch had to be carved for each letter of the alphabet. After the type was molded, a way had to be found to line up the separate letters into words and to lock them up tight in a frame so that the type would not slip. He might have to make

a special kind of ink. And he certainly had to have a press to push the paper down against the inked type.

"None of these things are to be found!" cried the inventor. "I have to make them all."

"Isn't there even a press that you can use?" asked Andrew. "People use presses to squeeze the juice out of grapes. And women use clothes-presses to take wrinkles out of dresses and shirts. Surely you can find a press to use."

Gutenberg said patiently, "Yes, but I shall need to have a different press for printing. I must find a carpenter who will make the kind I need."

As the partners said goodnight, each of them told the inventor that they hoped he would soon start making money.

Months passed. Then one afternoon Andrew went to the workshop to see what his partner was doing.

Gutenberg welcomed him with a shout. "I have it, Andrew! I have the metal I've been looking for. It's perfect metal for type."

Andrew looked at the bits of metal of many kinds lying on the table and at the iron pot hanging on a chain over the open fire. "Show me the metal, sir!" he said eagerly.

"Here it is!" Gutenberg held up a small bar. "I made it by mixing three metals together. This is easy to cast in a mold and yet is hard enough to stand pressure. Look, Andrew, I have made one mold, just to try out the metal. Now see where I have stamped it on this paper."

Andrew looked at the paper. It had ever so many prints of the figure 1 stamped on it. "You have made a beginning, Mr. Gutenberg. But why isn't the print blacker and clearer?"

Impatiently the inventor answered, "Oh, I have not yet found the right ink for metal type. First I must make my molds and carve the punches."

To do so took more months of work. The little strip to which the letter was fastened was easy to cut and to cast. But the letter itself was difficult. The face of each type had to be held by a stem with just the right slant and with certain ridges and notches. Again and again Gutenberg had to throw away the models he had made and start again.

Such waste was very expensive. Gutenberg had to borrow money. He had become too poor to pay his taxes. Worst of all was the impatience of his partners. They could not understand the inventor's problems. The only help they could give him was with the press.

Andrew took Gutenberg's design for a press to a carpenter. Nobody had ever seen anything like it before. It was very big and heavy. It had two thick posts held together by a heavy cross-beam on top. In the middle of the beam was a large screw turned by a handle. From the screw's lower end hung a very heavy block of smooth wood. This could be lowered and raised by turning the screw.

Between the two posts of the press a narrow bench was made to slide. It was to hold the frame in which the type was locked. First a sheet of paper was laid over the inked type. Then the big block could be screwed down to press the paper evenly against the type.

Andrew had the press taken to his house. His partners decided that no one was to see it until everything else was ready.

And now, another part of the invention was worked out. Andrew and the other partners were called to the shop to watch Gutenberg mold a piece of type.

First, Gutenberg held up a small bar of steel. At its top the metal had been carefully cut away to leave the letter S standing out clear. "This steel tool is the punch," said the inventor. "Watch it work!"

He placed the S face down on a thick, small bar of copper. Then with a hammer he gave the steel punch a sharp blow. The top sank deep into the soft copper and left a hollow in the shape of the letter S.

"What you see," he explained to his partners, "is the copper mold for the letter S. Now I'll cast the letter."

From a pot hanging over the fire Gutenberg dipped a small amount of hot metal. He poured it into the hollow just punched into the copper bar. When the metal cooled, he gently knocked it out of the mold, and there was a perfect letter S ready for use for printing.

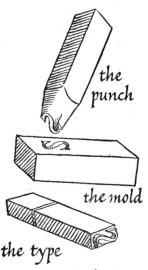

the punch

the mold

the type

"I can mold a thousand pieces of type for this letter in one day," said Gutenberg. "Already I have cut punches for half the alphabet. Now I must cut punches for the rest of the letters."

"What? Only for half of the alphabet in all this time?" cried one of the partners.

Gutenberg's face flushed with anger. But he said quietly, "Remember that each letter I carve must be of the same height, and so far as possible, of like thickness. To carve by exact measure takes time. You see I have to carve capitals and small letters—fifty-two punches in all. I have been working night and day. But once I finish the letters we can mold all the type we want."

THE RIGHT KIND OF INK

Not long after that Gutenberg was hard at work one afternoon when a boy burst into the shop. "Mr. Gutenberg," he panted, "your partner, Mr. Andrew, was taken sick and now is dead."

Gutenberg was shocked. This news brought not only grief but also fear. What about the press in Andrew's house? The people coming to the funeral would surely see it and ask about it. In haste he had the carpenter go to the house and take the press apart. People heard about that and said again that Gutenberg was working secret magic.

Not long after Andrew's death, the inventor sent word to his two other partners that he was ready to try a page of print. He had molded hundreds of each letter of the alphabet. In a wooden frame he had set up a page from a Latin grammar. The big press had been set up in his workshop. When the frame was locked and each letter brushed with ink, the bench was pushed in place between the heavy posts. Paper was laid over the frame.

Eagerly the partners watched the preparations. "Turn the screw!" Gutenberg called to his helper. "Lower the weight."

Down it came, gently and firmly pressing the paper against the type. At another command, the helper raised the weight again. With trembling fingers Gutenberg drew off the printed page and three heads bent over it.

The partners uttered cries of despair. They could hardly read a word. The letters were dim and smeared. Even a second and a third trial gave no better result. Here was another disappointment.

"This is too much!" cried one of the men. "Let us give up this costly business. It is a failure."

Gutenberg hardly seemed to hear. He was studying the printed page. "The trouble is only with the ink," he said calmly. "I see that I have not yet found the right mixture."

Although his partners stamped off in disgust, he began that very day to experiment with ink. For weeks he tried different mixtures. Nothing gave good results.

Then one day he went to a fine dinner. There he met an artist from the city of Venice in Italy. The visitor happened to say that many painters in Italy and Holland were using linseed oil to blend their colors. It gave smoothness to the paint.

Gutenberg's eyes grew big. "Linseed oil!" he said to himself. "That's what I'll try next."

When he had mixed the oil with lampblack, he had a smooth ink. It was thick, but not too thick. Carefully he brushed it over the type. When all was ready he lowered the weight.

The moment he took the page from the press, his heart sang with triumph. "At last!" he shouted. "The task is done!"

There before him was a page so clear that it could be read easily. Gutenberg stood thinking of the years of work behind that one page of print. The right metal for the type, the best metal for the molds, designs for the letters, the carving of the punches, the right mixture for the ink, and finally, the building of a press; all those things had had to be done. Now, at last, the invention of printing was complete.

PRINTED BOOKS AT LAST

Gutenberg's first important printing was a Latin Grammar. His partners came to watch the sheets coming off the press. Now they were pleased and excited.

"Teachers and schoolboys will be surprised to see these printed pages," said Gutenberg happily.

The moment the grammar was put on sale, the people of Strasbourg were wild with excitement. "What is this?" they cried. "These pages are not made from wood-blocks."

In a twinkling all the copies were sold.

The grammar was the only important book that Gutenberg printed in Strasbourg. He went back to Mainz and there his most important work began. In

the city of his birth he found a man willing to lend a large sum of money to start a printing business. His name was Johann Fust.

"We must work fast, Mr. Gutenberg," urged Fust. "Other men are at work on this invention also. One man in Holland has gone far. To make money we must be ahead of all the rest."

Gutenberg gazed into the distance and said, "Yes, but the important matter is to do everything well. I am making new patterns for the letters. Each page must be beautiful."

Fust shook his head. He had great respect for the inventor. But he had no patience with dreams. In haste, he rented a shop and began to have a press made. Both he and Gutenberg agreed that their work must be kept very secret. Their shop was the only one in Mainz not open to the street. Soon, here, as in Strasbourg, people began whispering that magic was going on.

Several workmen were hired to prepare molds, cut punches, and make type. One of the workmen was Peter Schoeffer. He not only learned quickly, but loved his work. Even when Gutenberg refused to accept a punch he had spent weeks in carving, Peter never complained.

"Yes, I see," he would say, "I have not made the slant of the stem quite right." Then he would try again.

64

Fust, however, had little patience with such carefulness. He was too eager to make money. When he found Peter Schoeffer so quick and clever, he paid him many favors. After a while he arranged marriage between his daughter and young Schoeffer.

It was decided that the first book to come off the press must be the Bible. That was what people wanted most of all.

After months had gone by, Fust came into the shop one day to ask, "Have you printed the Book of Genesis yet?"

"No," replied Gutenberg. "We started, but I did not like the size of the letters. They must be large like the letters used by the monks. Then the pages will be more beautiful."

Fust raved and shook his fist. He shouted that such a change meant that all the type would have to be destroyed and all the punches made over.

Gutenberg nodded calmly. "Yes, it is a pity. But one cannot always see beforehand. We must have a Bible as beautiful as those made by hand."

After more than two years of work the final printing began. The large letters were set in two columns on a wide page. The first letter of every chapter was drawn and colored by hand. Some of the pages were decorated like handmade Bibles. Gutenberg watched every page as it came off the press. If all the letters were not black and clear, he would tear up the page. Slowly the finished pages piled up. Two hundred copies of each page were printed.

DISAPPOINTMENT

"Now," said Gutenberg proudly to Fust, "we have printed the first volume of six hundred pages. The second volume will be of the same size."

Fust danced around in a fury. "Are you only half finished?" he shouted. "I've been paying out money for wages, metals, ink, and tools for more than four years and not one cent has been earned. How long do you expect me to wait?"

For a time Peter Schoeffer would argue with Fust. "Mr. Gutenberg is an artist," he would say. "Look how beautiful these pages are. He wants perfection."

But after Peter married Fust's daughter he changed his ideas. He began to feel that the work was taking too long and costing too much. Now and then Peter printed some small thing and sold it. But the master paid no heed to anything but the Bible.

When another year had gone by, John Fust came to Gutenberg. "Either you pay back a large part of the money I have loaned or else you must give the printing business to me."

Gutenberg stared at his partner in amazement. Then he turned to look at Peter Schoeffer. He had

taught Peter all he knew about printing, but now the
young man was a master. He was skilled enough to
carry on the work. All at once Gutenberg saw that
Fust and his son-in-law meant to finish printing the
Bible themselves. He saw that they meant to reap all
the profits from its sale.

"You have put money into this work," he said to
the two men, "but I have put my whole life into it. It
is I who have made printing possible. You know I
have no money, so how can I pay you?"

As he spoke the old inventor looked like a man
wounded unto death.

John Fust did not give in. In a court of law he brought his partner to trial for debt. Gutenberg knew that he could not win. He did not even go to the trial. The law court ruled that Fust was to have everything his money had bought—the press, the tools, and all that had been printed. And so the magnificent Bible designed and mostly printed by Gutenberg was finished, not by him, but by Fust and Schoeffer.

DESERVER
OF HIGHEST HONORS

Gutenberg was heartbroken. His only comfort was that his plan for the book was not changed. In one year it was ready for sale. When Fust took a number of copies to Paris no one could believe these beautiful books had been made on a machine. Every educated person in Europe was thrilled even to hear about them.

For a while Gutenberg had a small printing shop of his own. But soon the Archbishop of Mainz gave him a place in his household and a yearly sum of money. In Mainz he was treated with much honor. Before he died, he directed the printing of another Bible.

Fifty years after Fust finished the Gutenberg Bible, presses were at work in every country in Europe. In that time a million books were printed. Then books became so cheap that thousands of people could buy them and learn to read.

More and more people found it exciting to learn from books. Men who had something interesting to tell found it worth while to write it down. Now they knew that many people would read their printed books. So it was that the invention of printing helped to free people from ignorance.

John Fust and Peter Schoeffer and also an inventor in Holland claimed to have brought printing to their fellow men. But Johann Gutenberg's name will live forever as the man who was the real father of printing.

Near his tomb in Mainz was set up a small bronze sign which calls Gutenberg the "Inventor of the art of printing and deserver of the highest honors in every nation and tongue."

Talking Together

1. Look at each picture in the story carefully. They represent scenes of five hundred years ago. Name all the objects that you can see that are like objects you know now. Try to figure out from the story what the objects are that seem strange to you.

2. The story mentions grammar books and Bibles. How many different kinds of books do you know? There are cookbooks, books on radio, spelling, etc.

3. Why did people think magic was going on in the rooms where Gutenberg worked? Would you call his work anything like magic?

Working Together

1. Collect books, magazines, and newspapers in as many different languages as you can find. Then make an exhibit of these.

2. Soak small torn pieces of newspaper in a pail of water. When they are very soft spread them on a board and press the water out with another piece of wood. Then let the wet mass dry and you will have a thick piece of paper on which you can draw.

3. Notice all of the different people mentioned in the story. Make up something that one of them might have said, and when it is your turn see if the class can guess what person you are.

4. Bring to school the most beautiful book you can find at home or borrow from the library or from a friend. Tell the class why you think it is beautiful. Does a beautiful book have to have pictures?

To Do by Yourself

1. Write a title for each of the pictures in the story.

2. On page 57 start reading with the sentence that begins "Andrew took . . ." and continue through the sentence that ends ". . . by turning the screw." (See picture on page 63.) The sentences you have just read make a *paragraph*. A group of sentences written about one thing is called a *paragraph*. The one thing that all of the sentences tell or ask about is called the *topic* of the *paragraph*. We might call the *topic* of the *paragraph* you have just read "Gutenberg's first press," since all of the sentences describe the parts of his press.

What is the *topic* of the *paragraph* on page 48 that begins "After that, Johann spent . . ."? If you are not sure what the *topic* is, read each sentence by itself and think what each one tells about. Then decide what one thing all of the sentences tell about. That one thing is the *topic*.

What are the *topics* of these *paragraphs?*

The *paragraph* on page 45 beginning "Johann was . . ."

The *paragraph* on page 46 beginning "Grinning with . . ."

The *paragraph* on page 53 beginning "Young Gutenberg . . ."

3

FREE MAN

The Story of *LEONARDO DA VINCI*

Introduction. FREE MAN

ITALY is one of the lovely countries of the world. Its cities have many of the most beautiful buildings, paintings, and sculptures that men have ever made. The peaceful little towns on the low hills are framed in groves of olive trees. One would never guess what a stormy time this land has had.

For many hundred years Italy was divided into small states with different rulers. In each state there was a large town which was the center of government. That was where the ruler lived.

Because Italy was so divided, war was going on somewhere all the time. Suppose our country had no president or congress and that our big cities were centers of little separate governments. Imagine Chicago sending out an army to conquer St. Louis, or Boston and New York joining to defeat the troops of Philadelphia. Troubles like that were happening in Italy for hundreds of years.

No wonder the cities were built on hilltops for safety. No wonder they had high walls around them for defense. Public buildings and palaces were built with tall towers

74

from which a watchman could see an enemy coming. Because wars were so costly, high taxes kept workers and farmers poor. Only merchants and noblemen grew wealthy.

But there was one good thing about all this rivalry among cities. Everybody in each city wanted that city to be the center of learning and art. Therefore rulers and rich men spent money to encourage students, musicians, artists, and skilled workmen. After the year 1300, in spite of wars, Italy led the world in making beautiful materials and fine things in gold and silver. Also, the churches, palaces, and hospitals were the envy of Europe. Above all, painters were learning to paint lovelier pictures. When a great painting was finished, the citizens of the town would rush to admire it. Even the little street boys were proud of the artists.

The city of Florence led all other cities of Italy in every form of art. For many years the people of Florence chose their own governors. But at last a powerful merchant seized the government. He and his sons who followed him, however, loved the city. As time went on they spent great sums of money to make the city noble and full of joy. They hired dozens of artists and sculptors to paint pictures and make statues. When one of these merchant princes gave a festival, artists and musicians joined to make costumes, banners, and songs. On moonlit nights the city hummed with music. Young men strolled along the river singing and playing a small instrument called a lute.

The Story of
LEONARDO DA VINCI

TO THE MASTER'S STUDIO

ABOUT the year 1467 there came into Florence on horseback a man and a boy. As they crossed the bridge into the city, the boy cried out, "I see the great tower built by Giotto! I see the dome of the cathedral. Oh, this glorious city at last!"

Just then the horse he was riding stumbled. The man beside him said sternly, "Mind your horse, my son! Look! The street yonder is crowded. Take care!"

For a moment the boy bent down to speak softly to his steed. As he did so his long, fine, golden hair fell forward. But almost at once his eyes turned toward the big houses along the river and the tower of the public palace.

Presently the pair trotted into the courtyard of a large house. A servant hurried to take the bridles of the horses. He said, "Welcome, sirs. Your arrival is expected."

In another two minutes the travelers were seated in a big room hung with fine tapestries. The boy sat in a dreamlike silence while his father talked to their host.

"My son, Leonardo, has a gift for drawing," said the visitor. Then he gave a sigh. "He is interested in so many things: birds, butterflies, and any kind of

machine. What can one do with such a boy? He is now fifteen years old. 'Tis time he put his mind to something which will pay his living. I hope that here in Florence he can become a painter."

The host nodded. "True enough! And so, **as you** wrote me in your letter, you are taking him **to the** master's studio to learn painting."

"Yes, my friend. Tomorrow morning we go to **see** the master. Ah, if he will only accept Leonardo as a pupil, and let him stay in his house, and make him work!"

Leonardo seemed to pay no attention to this talk. But his heart was pounding. He knew it would be a wonderful thing to work under this great master.

Next morning he went with his father to the studio. To his joy the artist seemed to like the drawings he had brought.

"So you are Leonardo from the town of Vinci," said the artist. "You are indeed welcome to stay and work with us. We will see what you can do. Heaven knows there is plenty of work! Upstairs I have a little room in which you may sleep."

Quietly the boy thanked the artist. Then calmly he watched his father ride away. He knew his father was glad to have his puzzling son stay and work here.

"Come!" said the artist, taking the boy's arm and leading him to a group of workers. "I will put you in the hands of these youths who work in my studio. Young men, this is Leonardo da Vinci who has come to work here. Let him paint a flock of birds in the corner of that wall painting on which you work. We must see what he can do."

SO MUCH TO LEARN!

Thus began a wonderful life for the boy. The master saw at once that he could draw and paint better than any of the other helpers. He paid him well and laughed to see how the boy spent his money.

"Look at our Leonardo!" he said to the other youths. "He has the finest stockings, and a prince might envy that blue velvet cape of his."

"Indeed, sir," said one of the young men, "our Leonardo is very like a prince. He is so handsome and full of grace. His dancing and singing are the envy of all."

To another youth the master said, "Yesterday I saw you riding with Leonardo along the Arno River. Are you his special friend?"

"Nay, sir. Leonardo is the friend of all. Yet he depends on no one. He confides in no one. He goes his own way."

One evening, weeks later, the master thought of that remark. Returning from dinner with a rich noble, he saw a light burning in Leonardo's room and knocked at his door.

"What keeps you up so late, dear youth?" asked the master. " 'Tis long past midnight. 'Tis time you were in bed."

Rising politely to greet the master, Leonardo said that he was too deep in study to know the time. On his table lay a parchment scroll covered with figures. It was a book on mathematics. On the wall was pinned a chart of the heavens showing the location of stars and planets. Before him stood a little clay model of the clumsy cannon then used in war.

The young man tossed back his golden hair and said eagerly, "There is so much to learn and so little time to use what one learns!"

"Yes," said the master slowly, "but do you not set painting above all else; you who paint so divinely?"

Leonardo shook his head thoughtfully. "No, sir. Art is only one door into understanding. Science is another, and I long to open it a little wider. Men must learn the great laws which rule the sun and stars, the tides and the seasons."

ARTIST AND SCIENTIST

Florence in those days was a place where every man of talent worked hard. Carvers, woodworkers, sculptors, builders, and painters had more orders than they could fill. Not only the rulers, but men of wealth and heads of churches bought beautiful works of art as fast as they were finished. The sketches and studies for pictures which Leonardo made were snatched from the studio walls by eager buyers. His fame spread through the city. Yet for years he undertook no big work.

One sunny day a sculptor, coming from the ruler's palace, found Leonardo standing on the bridge across the Arno. The youth was staring at the birds flying around above him. When he did not return the gay greeting called out to him, the sculptor half-angrily shook Leonardo's shoulder.

"Why are you idling here on the bridge? You should be painting."

Still, Leonardo did not turn his head. "Just look at those birds, my friend!" he said softly. "See how in flight they move the tips of their wings up or down as they rise or descend. They must steer with their tails."

"Are you mad?" cried the sculptor in amazement. "Think of a great painter wasting his precious time watching birds!"

Now Leonardo turned and looked at his friend. "Is it mad to learn the secrets of this wonderful world?" he asked. "Perhaps if man understood the flight of birds, he too might find a way to fly."

The sculptor roared with laughter. "What a strange person you are! Last Thursday I saw you coming from the deep woods all dirty and torn from climbing over rocks. Yet that night at the palace ball you looked more splendid than anyone else. And you sang a song you had composed which drew much praise. Why must you dip into so many things? Isn't painting enough?"

But Leonardo was watching the birds again. With a snort of disgust the sculptor went on his way.

THE UNFINISHED WORK

As a matter of fact, Leonardo had just consented to undertake a big painting. It was ordered by the monks of a monastery near Florence. At last he stood, with pencil in hand, before a big sheet of paper on the studio wall. Excitement seized all the other young men in the place. Gathering around him, they asked, "What scene from the Scriptures will you choose?"

He answered that it took time to know what was worth painting. And for weeks he put only a few faint lines on the paper. Then one morning there he was, hard at work! As the other artists came in laughing and joking, they saw him and grew silent. One after another stole up to watch that sure pencil. Leonardo was sketching a crowd of people who were all looking in one direction.

No one dared to ask him what he had in mind. Each man had a different guess. But to the disappointment of them all, Leonardo left his work again. What was he doing, they asked one another.

Reports about him were brought to the studio. "I saw Leonardo today," said a merchant. "He was sketching in his notebook at the market place." Often he was seen riding over the hills on his horse. One man had found him talking with the workmen who were building a new wing on the huge Pitti Palace.

No one knew, however, that Leonardo had come away from the Pitti Palace with a new idea. He had watched the builders as they moved heavy stones. He believed those stones could be lifted into place by means of ropes pulled over wheels. For weeks he tried to figure out how big the wheels must be and how thick the rope to lift a stone weighing five hundred pounds. He sketched his invention over and over until he had made a drawing scientifically exact.

No wonder that nearly a year went by before the big drawing for the monastery was finished. Now it was ready to be painted. Dozens of artists flocked to the studio to gaze at the beautiful sketch. Leonardo had used a gold pencil and even the shadows had a golden tone.

It was a picture of the Wise Men coming to adore the Christ Child. He sat in His Mother's arms on a

kind of throne of light. Both looked down with loving calm upon the crowds coming to worship Them.

"Look at the faces of those people!" a famous artist exclaimed. "How does Leonardo show such hope and such wonder in them?"

"See what strange rocks he has in the background!" remarked another visitor. "And the tree near the Madonna. Ah, never was such beauty!"

Far from his picture, talking little, stood Leonardo. In his rose velvet tunic and silk cap, he looked very handsome. But, though he smiled politely at his visitors, he did not seem to delight in their praise. He had an air of seeing something far away.

So he was. That morning he had been out at the stables petting his horse. As the horse pawed the ground in his eagerness for a gallop, his master had begun to dream of making a statue of a horseman on a wild, strong steed.

Meeting his friend the sculptor on his way home, he said, "Florence is filled with sculptured horses in bronze and marble. Yet none of them has the spirit of a horse like mine."

Filled with this thought, he spent all his time sketching horses in every kind of motion. Not a moment did he give to painting the picture for the monastery. Again and again the monks came, urging him to finish the work. They brought gifts of wine. They begged and pleaded. Leonardo was polite and charming, but would promise nothing. Finally, he advised the monks to get a young artist friend of his to do the painting.

"But why is he like that?" the disappointed monks asked the master of the studio. "Leonardo has drawn something that is so beautiful. Why will he not paint his picture?"

"I know not," was the answer. "Perhaps in his drawing, Leonardo has given all that he can to this one piece of art. Already the young men who have seen it are painting better than they did before. Leonardo da Vinci has to find new ways to see things and to do things."

Shortly after this Leonardo went away to live in Milan. He had been invited there by the ruler, whose name was Sforza. All Florence was sad when he went away. For fifteen years everyone in the city had watched the young artist and wondered about him.

Just as he left, a man came from Rome to choose an artist to paint pictures for the Pope. He asked at once to see Leonardo's work. A young man who had studied with Leonardo said that he had left almost nothing in Florence.

"Then why is he so famous, so praised, and so beloved?" cried the Roman. "What has he done?"

Quickly the youth replied, "What has a rose tree done that we should praise it? It grows freely into a thing of beauty. And Leonardo, too, has shown us what it is to be free. He is no slave to rules in painting and no slave to men of wealth and power. Never has he painted a picture just to please them. His task is to show us in many ways the wonderful secrets of nature, the works of God."

In the meantime, Leonardo galloped north on the horse he loved. His servant rode behind him. The way lay through a wide plain. Just south of the towering Alps Mountains, near a region of lovely lakes, stands the city of Milan. It was built above swampy lands cut by canals and many little streams.

At last the traveler and his servant reached the streets of the town and rode up the steep path to the duke's castle. Servants brought in his saddlebags. Two noblemen took him at once to the duke.

Sforza, the ruler, had grave and gentle manners. He welcomed Leonardo as if he had been a prince. "Your house is ready, sir," said he. "I hope you will be happy here."

Leonardo fumbled among his pile of sketchbooks and notebooks. "I have brought you a gift, your excellency," he said. "I made this lute for you." The instrument was shaped like the head of a magic horse. Leonardo struck the lute with his long fingers and it gave off a sweet, sad tone. The duke was deeply pleased with the gift.

The artist from Florence was given servants and horses and splendid clothes for his life at court. In return, he had to plan the festivals and paint portraits of some of the fine court ladies. He enjoyed working out costumes and special lighting for the balls. Yet he saw that he was not so free to do as he pleased as he had been in Florence.

THE STATUE

Sforza was always saying in a gentle, respectful way that he hoped Leonardo would paint a beautiful picture or make a great statue which would bring fame to Milan. One evening the duke found the artist telling stories to a group of laughing courtiers. He drew him aside.

"An idea has come to me," said Sforza, "that you might make a statue of my father."

This was the man who had seized the government of Milan some thirty years before and handed it on to his son.

Leonardo's eyes sparkled. "A conqueror on a mighty steed!" he exclaimed. "Often have I dreamed of such a thing."

From then on he began to plan the statue. He had chosen a number of handsome youths to help him in his studio. They adored him, but most of them had little talent.

90

Milan was a place of pleasure, and no one, except farmers and poor people, did any work. There were no busy artists in Milan as there were in Florence. The wealthy nobles and landowners cared only for riding to the hunt and going to balls at the castle. Yet they were proud to have Leonardo among them. They missed him when he shut himself up in his studio for weeks at a time. They almost envied the young men who helped him.

After lonely hours in his room, the artist would come out and talk to the students about the statue he wanted to make.

"Sforza, the conqueror, must be shown moving forward into action. His steed should be plunging as if in battle with front feet in the air."

"But, master," cried one of the youths, "if all the weight of horse and rider are on the steed's hind legs, will there not be danger of the statue's falling?"

"Exactly," said Leonardo thoughtfully. "That is the problem that worries me. Perhaps the forefeet should rest upon a fallen enemy."

He made hundreds of drawings of the horse and many models of the statue. Now and then the curious nobles would come in to see the final model he had begun to make in clay. They talked about it so much that long before it was finished its fame had gone to the far corners of Italy.

Years went by. Then one day a troop of servants and porters lifted the covered statue into a big cart and took it up to the castle courtyard. There it was set up and uncovered. Most of the townsfolk were there to see. They had heard much about the great statue. Now, after years of waiting, Leonardo's horse and rider were here in the courtyard.

Shouts of admiration arose. "Never was such a statue!" "Both man and horse are alive with fierce strength!"

Pride in that horseman of clay never grew less. The visitors to Milan were always taken to see it. People begged Sforza to have it cast in bronze. But although workers in bronze all over Italy were asked to undertake the task, none would do so. Casting that huge figure on the galloping horse was thought impossible.

THE INVENTOR

Whatever else Leonardo was doing, he never stopped his studies in science. He invented a powerful shovel for digging ditches and canals, and also terrible tools of war. When his pupils looked at his notebooks, they found all sorts of scientific drawings, but they could not read one word of the secret notes.

"What kind of language does he use?" they asked one another. "We can understand nothing of it. We cannot read it."

No wonder. Leonardo was left-handed. Besides that, he wrote from right to left so that each word and each letter was written backward and could only be read in a mirror. The Italian word for horse is *cavallo* and he wrote it

O⅃⅃AVAƆ

Over and over again he made drawings of a thing that looked like a giant bird. One afternoon he looked up from his notes and said aloud, "I know now that men can fly like birds. Some day they will make a machine to carry them freely through the air."

For a moment the young men stared at their beloved master. Finally they could not help bursting into laughter. When he left the studio a little later, they said to one another, "Our master is mad!"

"Once he said the earth moves around the sun. Now he tells us men will fly like birds!"

"Is it magic that he studies?"

Many ignorant folk thought that the tall, silent man was a magician. But Sforza did not. He always listened eagerly when Leonardo talked of science. The duke wanted to use this man of knowledge to help him hold his land. The king of France was threatening war. And the people of Milan were almost ready to rise up against Sforza. "Why should we who are poor have to pay heavy taxes while the rich live in idle luxury?" they cried. Sforza wished to calm them by making things better.

He asked Leonardo to have his powerful shovel made, and then direct the draining of the unhealthy swamps. He also begged him to draw up a plan to give the people better houses and wider streets. For defense, in case of war, he wished the castle walls to be made stronger.

With interest and energy Leonardo plunged into this work. He proved that science could solve many problems of living and fighting.

94

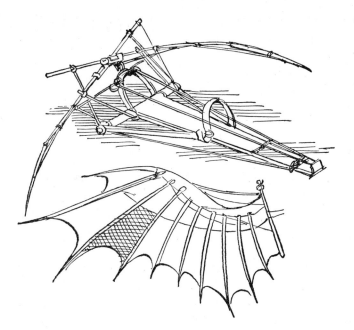

THE SECRET MACHINE

When Leonardo was not directing workmen, he was completely absorbed in another invention. It was so secret that no one was allowed to step into the big room at the top of the house where hammering and pounding could be heard day and night.

"He makes a magic machine up there!" whispered his pupils.

Sforza only shrugged when he heard this. But he would have been amazed to see the thing Leonardo was putting together. Great wings of silk, stretched over thin strips of wood, filled the big room from floor to ceiling. Hour by hour the inventor tried to find out how the weight of a man could be held in air by wings.

Yes, more than four hundred years ago Leonardo tried to prove that man could conquer the air. He did not prove it because he could not. Even though what he built was a kind of glider to sail in the wind, there were none of the light materials known today for him to use. Yet the fact that he knew men could fly was handed on through hundreds of years. Since the time of Leonardo men kept searching for a way to fly, until at last they found it. Even his notes and drawings helped their search.

THE LAST SUPPER

At last Leonardo granted Sforza's wish to have great paintings in Milan. He presented him with a beautiful Madonna. Then he undertook an order for a monastery. The monks wanted a fresco for the wall of the room where they ate their meals. A fresco is painted directly on the wall after a fresh coat of plaster has been spread upon it. Italians were fond of doing frescoes and knew the kind of paint mixture which would stick to the plaster without cracking.

Month after month the artist made sketches. He dreamed and thought. Finally, he chose to picture that moment in the life of Jesus when, during His last week on earth, He sat with His disciples at supper. After talking with them for a long time, He said, "Verily, verily I say unto you that one of you shall betray me."

In Leonardo's picture the disciples gaze at one another in surprise, grief, and fear. Judas, the guilty one, wears a look of terrible sorrow. Peter has sprung to his feet. Only the beloved disciple, John, and Jesus are calm at this awful moment.

Slowly the drawing was finished, all except the head of Jesus.

At the monastery Leonardo prepared the plaster and began to transfer the unfinished picture to the wall. "I am using a new mixture for the paint and plaster," he told his youthful helpers. "If it proves good, other painters can use it."

When at last the fresco was finished, and the head of Jesus painted, men saw a face that was filled with a love and wisdom beyond that of even the noblest human being. People stood before *The Last Supper* as if they were in church. Many kneeled before it. They asked one another, "How could Leonardo have painted this picture? It is as if he had seen the face of Our Lord."

Sforza's courtiers never tired of talking of both the picture and the artist. They had seen Leonardo make festivals beautiful and gay. They had watched him direct the work of strengthening the castle walls. They knew of his inventions. As a teller of tales and player on the lute he had charmed everyone. Yet this same man could paint *The Last Supper* as if he had thought of nothing else.

DISASTERS

Hardly was the masterpiece finished when the war Sforza had feared broke out. The French king brought troops to storm Milan. After a terrible struggle, Sforza was defeated in battle. Then he was captured and taken as a prisoner to France. He ended his days in a dungeon.

To escape the war Leonardo left Milan. First in one city and then in another he studied and worked. But he was not happy and made up his mind to return to Florence.

One day he was resting at a village from his long ride. Suddenly a youth who had been one of his pupils in Milan galloped up to the inn.

"Master," cried the young man, "I bring you cruel news. The French soldiers have destroyed your great statue in the castle courtyard. Oh, master, if only it had been cast in bronze. Then they could not have broken it to pieces."

For a moment Leonardo bowed his head. Ten years of work ruined in a few moments! Then he looked at the youth and said calmly, "The soldiers could not destroy my joy in creating the statue, nor the joy of others in seeing it."

In a shocked tone the youth said, "You do not grieve?"

"Nay," said Leonardo, "let the past go. There are other things to do now."

In Florence he was received like a royal person. He hired a studio, and there he welcomed his friends. To their joy he soon began an altarpiece for a group of monks. It was a study of the Madonna with the Christ Child and St. Anne.

When it was finished, one man wrote to a friend, "The whole city was stirred, and you might have thought you saw a procession on a feast day."

Shortly after that Leonardo left Florence. He had accepted a strange mission. This time all his knowledge of the science of war was called into use.

A handsome, brave, and powerful young man was leading his armies up and down Italy to conquer states and cities for the Pope. Leonardo joined his troops to make new machines of war and to help restore waterways of conquered cities. From town to town, and camp to camp, they traveled. But when at last the powerful young man was killed, Leonardo went back to Florence.

"I will make a picture showing how terrible war is!" said he. And he drew a fierce and bloody battle scene.

At once it was bought for the wall of a public building. Again, as with his fresco in Milan, the artist tried something new. He tried a kind of paint which needed heat to set the colors. When the painting was finished and on the wall, friends and pupils came to help him. They lit fires in iron pots and set them close to the painting. Joyously they waited.

Then a cry rang out, "Look, master! Oh, Heaven, let not this thing happen!"

The glowing colors were running into one another. In the big, cold room the heat from the pots had not been great enough to dry the paint. In an hour the masterpiece was ruined.

Still another disaster happened to Leonardo's work. On a visit to Milan he went to the monastery to look once more at *The Last Supper*. One of his pupils, who was with him, stood in silent wonder before the scene. Hearing a low groan, he turned quickly to find the painter rubbing his finger along the edge of the fresco.

"It is peeling off!" cried Leonardo. "The paint mixture I used will not last. Nothing can save it."

He was right. Today this picture, one of the greatest in the world, is but a pale ghost.

A HARVEST FOR OTHERS

Leonardo's last years were full of wanderings.
For a time he was in Rome. Later he returned to Florence, and there something happened which brought
him deep happiness. A merchant asked the artist to
paint a portrait of his wife, Mona Lisa. As soon as
he saw the lady seated in his studio, he knew that here
was a face at which he could look forever. It was so
quiet, so wise, so full of secrets.

For months he worked on the portrait, changing a
shadow under the dreamy eyes, adding a deeper rose
to the half smiling lips. Often the merchant protested,
"Is the picture not finished yet?" But the answer was

always, "No, not yet." People near the studio said they could hear musicians playing there to entertain Mona Lisa as she posed.

At last Leonardo accepted an invitation from the king of France to stay at his court. When he left Florence he took with him the portrait of Mona Lisa, for he could not bear to part with it. Now it hangs in the great museum of Paris, and every visitor to the French capital goes to see it. Writers and poets have praised this portrait beyond all others. Because Leonardo painted her, Mona Lisa, the quiet Florentine, is one of the most famous women of the world.

Leonardo da Vinci was painter, inventor, musician, and man of science. One of his fellow Italians who knew him said of him: "He was so perfected in mind and body, that to whatever hard things he turned his mind, he solved them with ease."

Here was a man like a sower of seed who let other people reap the harvest. He was not a leader of men nor a doer of noble deeds. Yet during all these hundreds of years his name has held a kind of magic. For he obeyed only an inner voice which said, "Create! Create! Show others the way!" Even when his wonderful works of art were destroyed, he still obeyed that voice.

Talking Together

1. Here are groups of words that tell what you might see in a picture. Describe these pictures clearly so that others might understand what they mean.

> towns framed in groves of olive trees
> dome of the cathedral
> courtyard of a large house
> building a new wing on the palace

2. Why was there so much war in Italy for so long a time? How did the cities protect themselves against their enemies?

3. What kind of work is done by each of the following?

> woodworkers   sculptors
> builders   painters   scientists

4. What is the difference between sketches, studies for pictures, and finished paintings?

Working Together

1. The story of Leonardo is divided into eleven sections, each with its own title. Divide the class into eleven committees. Then each committee can:

   a. Write titles for all of the pictures in its section

   b. Plan a dramatization of the most interesting part of the section

   c. Write one or two important questions about the section to ask the rest of the class

   d. Decide what contribution it could make to a bulletin board on Leonardo

2. Add to the picture dictionary begun in Unit I.

3. Look in encyclopedias, *National Geographic* magazines, and other books and magazines for pictures of the beautiful cities of Italy. Bring as many as you can to school for an exhibit.

4. Try to find out if anyone in your community has been to Italy. What questions would you like to ask that person about Florence, Milan, Rome, and other parts of Italy?

5. Plan a booklet on Leonardo to which the whole class will make contributions. You will need to discuss exactly what you want to put in it and just how those things are to be done. Decide also what you will do with the booklet when it is finished.

To Do by Yourself

1. Leonardo was an unusual man because he could create so many different things better than other men. Make a list of all the things which your story tells you Leonardo made. Then see if you can add to this list by reading more about Leonardo da Vinci in encyclopedias or books you might find in the library.

2. Try writing some secret notes like Leonardo's. Write some words from right to left with the letters written backwards. Can you read them in a mirror when your paper is held before it?

3. Find a map of Italy in a geography. Locate Florence, Milan, and Rome.

4 GREAT INVENTOR

The Story of *JAMES WATT*

Introduction. GREAT INVENTOR

IT is only a little over 200 years since George Washington was born. Yet in that time there have been more changes in the way people live and work than in all the thousands of years which went before.

Suppose a magician whisked us back to the time of our first President. Let us spend a day with a New York businessman.

When the man gets up one cold morning, a servant lights a fire in the fireplace and brings him a pitcher of hot water. The man washes in a bowl placed on a stand. Then he puts on clothes which have all been made by hand. His stockings were knitted by his wife, and his new shoes were made by a cobbler.

After breakfast the man starts on a business trip to Philadelphia. A servant brings horses from the stable and rides with his master down to the wharf. The servant then leads the master's horse home, and the businessman gets aboard a small sailboat which will take him across the Hudson River. This part of the trip takes more than an hour. At the landing place, with other passengers, he climbs into a coach drawn by four horses. The coach bounces and rolls over the rough road.

At sunset the passengers leave the coach to spend the night in a tavern. It is lighted by oil lamps and candles. Everything that is in it has been made by hand. The next morning the businessman rides on to Philadelphia.

Now suppose that the man could be whisked into the world of today. Let us see how he travels from Philadelphia back to New York. He is seated in a warm, comfortable train as he speeds over the country. Then the train goes under the river, and in a few minutes it reaches the station. The trip has taken him about two hours.

To explain such changes the businessman of 175 years ago would have to learn about many great inventions. In early days, men had only a few helpers aside from beasts of burden. One of these was the wind which filled sails. Another was the waterfall which turned mill wheels. In those days, human hands made everything.

Think how long it must have taken to spin threads and weave cloth by hand. The first modern inventions were machines for spinning and weaving. As soon as a way was found to drive those machines by water power, many spinners and weavers began to work together under one roof. That was the beginning of factories.

Machines driven by water power could turn out far more cloth in a day than could be made by hand. That was a big gain. But scientists were studying how to use another kind of power. This power was steam.

Even children knew that when water boiled, the steam could lift the lid of a teakettle. Scientists said, "If a little bit of steam can lift the lid of a pot, a great deal of steam can do far more."

An Englishman named Newcomen was the first to make steam do useful work. He knew that flooded coal mines needed a powerful pump to empty them. When water gushed out of springs far below the earth, workmen could not dig coal. All of the water could not be pumped out by hand. In 1705, after years of work, Newcomen made an engine that ran by steam and joined it to a pump.

The clumsy engine used up too much steam. To keep the boiler going, $16,000 worth of coal was burned in one year. Scientists, however, were thrilled that a way had been found to make steam work, and inventors in many lands began trying to make a better engine. Yet years went by before anyone succeeded.

The Story of
JAMES WATT

A BRIGHT LAD

IN the lowlands of Scotland is a small town at the mouth of the river Clyde. There the Watt family lived. The town had a fine harbor. At the big docks, sailing ships from Ireland, France, and America landed their cargoes. Then they reloaded with provisions and cloth. Often, ships which leaked or had other troubles were repaired by Mr. Watt. He was a skilled carpenter and had a shop near the docks.

Almost every morning one of the workmen at the shop would call out, "Well, here comes the little lad! Good day, Jamie!"

From the time James Watt could walk down from
the cottage, he spent hours in his father's shop. The
older he grew the more interested he became in all
that went on there.

His father would say to Mrs. Watt, "What questions Jamie asks! Already he knows all the tools I use."

Mrs. Watt would sigh, "If only our little son were
not so delicate! He cannot seem to grow strong."

Since the boy was not well enough to go to school,
his father taught him arithmetic, and his mother taught
him to read and to spell. He was quick at his lessons.

One day the captain of a ship came to the cottage to talk business with Mr. Watt. James greeted the man politely, then seated himself on the floor in front of the fireplace. On that warm spring morning no fire was burning, and the boy began making chalk marks on the smooth hearthstone.

"So this is your eldest son, Mr. Watt," the captain said. "How old is he?"

"Eight years old," replied Mr. Watt.

"Eight!" cried the captain. "Why isn't he in school, sir, instead of idling away time at home?"

Quietly the father answered, "See what my son is doing, captain, before you call him an idler."

The visitor strode to the fireplace and looked down. There in chalk on the hearth were circles, squares, and arithmetic problems neatly worked out.

With a low whistle the captain said, "Forgive me, Mr. Watt. Your son knows more than most boys of his age. I see he has good teaching at home."

James looked up smiling. "I'm going to school soon, sir, and I'm going to work in Father's shop, too."

LEARNING A TRADE

As he grew older, James went to school and also worked in his father's shop. But he was happier in the shop. The schoolboys teased him and called him names because he was not strong enough to play some of their games. On the other hand, the workmen in the shop were his friends. They taught him to make little things needed in their work, and they urged him to build small models of their machines. Once he made a tiny copy of a crane, the big machine used for unloading ships.

"That's a clever thing, Jamie!" the workmen said. "For a small lad you know much about machinery. You are a great help to us."

When James went to the grammar school, which is like our high school, his mother was delighted by his good reports. "I hope, son, that you can go to Glasgow to the university. You would do well there."

That was James's wish also. But in the year 1753, when he was seventeen, his mother died. Soon afterward his father talked with him about his future.

"My boy," said Mr. Watt, "some of my business plans have failed, and I have no money to send you to college. I fear you must start to earn your own living."

So James went up the river Clyde to Glasgow to find work. Before long he found a shop where he learned to make spectacles and telescopes. He stayed with his aunt and liked the visitors who came to her pleasant home.

Among the visitors who came to his aunt's home was a professor of science at the university. One day the professor said to James, "What would you like to do for a living?"

At once the youth replied, "I'd like to make tools for scientists to use, sir. But in Glasgow there is no shop where I can learn the trade."

"True, my boy. But why not go to London? I'll give you a letter to a Scotsman there who is in that very business."

Soon after that, James took the twelve-day horse-back trip to London. He gave the professor's friend the letter. But the man had no work for him and could only send him to other shops. At last James found a

master willing to teach him tool-making. But he had to pay the master one hundred dollars and promise to do all sorts of odd jobs in the shop.

James had little of his savings left for food. As time went on he grew thin and ill. Yet in one year he learned so much that he felt he could set up a shop of his own. With a fine kit of tools he went back home.

"Now," he said proudly to his father, "as soon as I get rested and strong I mean to have my own shop in Glasgow."

"Splendid, James," said Mr. Watt. "You have **good** friends there who will help you."

THE DISCOVERY

James found his father's words to be true. At the university one of the professors hired him to mend and clean instruments. He also gave him a room in which to work. In his spare time James studied science. Many of the younger teachers became his friends.

Within a few years James opened his own shop and even hired workmen. Then he felt he could afford to marry. The girl of his choice was named Peggy. She had a gay laugh, a pretty face, and a generous nature. The two were very happy.

One evening a science teacher came to dinner with the young Watts. James said to him, "Isn't it a pity that so many coal mines are closing down because they are flooded? Few mine owners can afford Newcomen's engine."

"Well," said the teacher, "although Newcomen did show us the way to use steam, his invention isn't very useful. His engine is not only expensive to run, but it is always breaking down. If only some inventor would make a good engine, he would do the world a great service."

Only a few days after that James was called over to the college. He was wanted in the room where many models of inventions were set up for study. James hurried toward the room.

"Look here, young Watt," said the professor in charge, "we've just received a small model of Newcomen's engine. It won't work. I thought you might be clever enough to repair it and to get it going."

Watt's gray eyes grew big with interest. "I'd like to try, sir, better than anything on earth."

For weeks the young man did little but study the model. He took it apart; cleaned and oiled it. He saw how each part worked and how all the parts worked together. Then one day he rushed to the professor. "I've got the engine going!" he cried. "Come and see!"

Ten minutes after the professor arrived, however, the engine stopped. "It's used up all the water in the boiler!" cried James in surprise. "There's something wrong in that."

Over and over again the same thing happened. James used up so much coal to heat the boiler that he finally had to give up running the engine. What was its great fault? Again he studied it part by part.

Then Watt settled down to find whatever he could from books. He read everything that he could find about engines. He even studied Italian and German to discover what inventors in those countries had been doing. With his scientific friends he talked over the problem. Whenever one of them came to dinner, he would say, "How could an engine work without using so much steam and without needing so much coal?"

His wife, Peggy, would say with a laugh, "You don't even know you're eating my good pudding. You think of nothing except that old engine."

"Yes," his friends would say jokingly, "perhaps James thinks he's going to do what nobody has done yet, make a really good steam engine."

"No," smiled Watt, "but I can't rest till I find out what ails this invention. I'm trying all sorts of ways to discover how steam behaves."

One Sunday afternoon in May, 1765, he was out walking by himself. Many people were strolling about the streets of Glasgow. But the young man saw no one. He was thinking about the way to make a steam engine work right. All at once a thrill went through him from head to foot.

"I've got it!" he said to himself. "There must be another part to the engine. Newcomen used only one cylinder, and there must be two! There must be an extra cylinder to cool the steam after it is used. Then, the main cylinder will stay hot!"

In great excitement he rushed home. "Oh, Peggy, I wish it weren't Sunday!" he shouted to his surprised wife. "I want to try something out in the shop right now."

"Jamie!" she laughed. "No proper Scotsman even dreams of working on Sunday."

THE INVENTION

Early next morning Watt began to rig up a model to try his great idea. But he had to make all the parts by hand. Day after day he hammered and pounded and fitted pieces of metal together. He rushed all over Glasgow to find metals, and pipes, and tools. The workmen at his shop had to run his business as well as they could. For James could not pay attention to anything except his model.

He was sitting one noon with a big tin tube on his lap, trying to decide where a pipe should be fitted to it. All at once he looked up to see his best friend, a scientist, coming into the shop with Peggy.

"We're here to make you come to dinner," said the man gaily. "Take off that old leather apron! What are you doing there anyway, nursing that roll of tin as if it were a baby? How about your engine?"

"Just you wait!" answered Watt. "I'm finishing a model that will surprise you. This engine won't need a thousand dollars' worth of coal a month to run it. No sir! This one isn't going to waste steam!"

His friend looked excited. "How did you plan it? Where is it?"

"You'll see it some day," said James, smiling. Then he turned to his wife. "Peggy, please lend me your thimble. It will do nicely to close an important little pipe."

Peggy hoped every week that her husband would tell her he had finished his model. But progress was slow. It was almost impossible to find either the right materials or the skilled workmen he needed. Besides, he had to try out many different ways of putting the parts together. No sooner was one small model almost complete than he saw how he could make a better one.

He had much encouragement from a man interested in coal mines. The moment this man received Watt's letter describing his invention, he saw it was very important. He begged Watt to build a full-sized model.

But Watt could not spend all his time on such a task. He had to support his wife and children. His shop no longer earned enough money, and he had to take up a different kind of work.

What Watt did was to plan how canals should be dug, and where they should go. Both city governments and private companies hired him. He had great success in this new work. And yet in his spare time he kept right on working at his invention.

In four years he had the big full-sized model ready. It was far from perfect. But when he tested it, it worked well and proved beyond a doubt that his idea was right. Then he set off for London, saying to his wife, "I have to ask the British government for a patent."

This meant that the government would give him a written paper protecting him by law so that nobody else could make or sell his invention without paying him.

THE PARTNERSHIP

On his way back from London, Watt stopped off at Birmingham. This town, in the middle of England, was famous for its factories. There the inventor met the man at the head of the city's largest factory. Matthew Boulton was his name.

Boulton's factory with its 600 workmen turned out all sorts of beautiful things in metal. The machines ran by water power. But often in summer water was scarce. Boulton had wondered if a pump, driven by steam, could force water back into the pond after it had been used. If it could, then the water could be used again and again. He did not think much of Newcomen's clumsy and costly engine. But after one glance at Watt's drawings of his model, Boulton was deeply interested.

"This is indeed a happy meeting, Mr. Watt," said he. "You must stay at my house. We will talk about your engine, and you shall see my factory."

Boulton was handsome, successful, and eager for new ideas. He liked the tall, shy Scotchman at once. The two men found they could share jokes as well as talk about the use of steam power.

"We ought to join together in making this engine for sale," said Boulton warmly. "You have a wonderful invention. I have a factory. Why, my dear sir, your engine could help the whole world."

Watt was thrilled at such words from a man who knew so well what he was talking about. He promised to go into partnership with Boulton.

Watt returned to Glasgow with great hopes for the future. Yet it took him four years to wind up his work on the canals and finish some useful tools he had invented.

During this time his wife Peggy died. Watt was very sad as he got ready to move to Birmingham. At last, however, in the spring of 1774, he and his children moved to the big English city.

Now for the first time, James Watt could give his heart and mind to his great work. Boulton paid him a regular salary and gave him materials and the help of skilled workmen. It was not long before he had built the kind of engine he had long dreamed about. A mine owner in western England came to see it and bought it right away.

Watt and Boulton both went to the mine to have the engine set up. Stories about the new invention had been printed in the newspapers. When the day came to start the engine and connect it with the big mine pump, a huge crowd was on hand. Mine owners from near and far were there to watch, and a newspaperman ran around asking questions and taking notes.

For nights Watt had not been able to sleep. He was very anxious about this first trial before a crowd. But once the engine was started, it worked the pump with such power that streams of water were forced out of the flooded mine. Cheers went up, and Watt gave a sigh of relief. Then at last he could bear to look around. He saw that the mine owners were amazed and delighted about the power of the new engine.

Turning to Matthew Boulton, who was beaming with great pride, Watt said, "Do you know why these mining men believe in our big, smoky monster?

It is because it makes a horrible noise. They think that the more noise it makes, the more power it has!"

Boulton laughed. "All the same, my friend, the Watt engines are going to be ordered for mines in both England and Scotland."

And so they were. In those days each engine had to be set up at the mine where it was to be used. A few of its parts were made in the Boulton factory. Other parts were made in other factories and brought to the mine. At first, Watt himself had to see that every engine was put together in just the right way. Later, Boulton hired a very skilled and clever man to help do this work. Then the inventor had time to work on improvements.

In a few years Watt married again and settled in a pleasant house in Birmingham not far from the factory. Many famous scientists lived in the city. They had a club and invited Watt to join it. He loved the evenings of good talk at the club meetings. Although he was very shy, he delighted the others by his stories, his learning, and his sense of fun.

Watt never stopped inventing ways to make the steam engine work better. Finally he made new improvements which doubled the power of the engine. The first of Watt's engines was used only for pumping water out of mines. But the improved model could do many kinds of work.

Boulton saw the value of these changes even more clearly than his friend did. "This last engine of yours," he said in triumph, "—why, there is no end to its uses. It is a marvel!"

Watt's newest model was first set up in London. A large flour mill was built in that city to be run by steam power. Engines were to work big cranes for unloading sacks of wheat from boats and for lifting them into the mill. Engines ran the rollers which ground wheat into flour. They also ran the big flour sifters. Almost all the work in the mill was done by machines driven by engines. Boulton, who had put money into building the mill, helped with all the plans. Every engine, of course, was Watt's new model.

When at last all was ready, and the engines were humming, Londoners flocked to see the big machines doing the work that men had always done. Mill owners from many towns went over the whole building to watch the work. They thought the mill one of the world's wonders.

PROGRESS FOR THE WORLD

One day about three years later, Boulton and Watt were in the Birmingham factory talking over plans. All at once a messenger burst into the office. He had hurried by stagecoach from London. "Gentlemen!" he gasped, "I have bad news. The mill has burned to the ground!"

Both Boulton and Watt lost thousands of dollars because of that fire. But the engines had proved what they could do. One by one, other millers began to order them from Boulton's factory.

By this time, Watt's fame had spread from factory owners and scientists to all sorts of people. It was plain that a new power was ready not only to do all kinds of work, but to work anywhere. Factories using water power had to close in a very dry season or in winter when streams were frozen. Moreover, it was not always possible to find a waterfall in a suitable place for a mill or factory. The steam engine, on the other hand, could be set up wherever it was needed.

Many spinning and weaving machines were changed to run by steam power instead of water power. Soon other factories put in steam-driven machines.

One day Watt's son rushed into his father's work-room. "Father!" he cried, "have you heard what your engine is going to run next? Some people are talking of building steamboats!"

At first the inventor thought this was nonsense. But it was not long before he found that the report was true. The best kind of steamship was finally built by the American inventor, Robert Fulton, in the year 1807. Driven by Watt's engine, the famous boat, the *Clermont*, steamed up the Hudson River against the current. After that, many people knew that little by little steamboats would take the place of sailing ships.

In 1825 the first railway was built in England, and a locomotive went chugging along the rails. The powerful engine with its big boiler had been built according to the ideas Watt had worked out. In the next forty years, hundreds of miles of railroads were built in Europe and America. People were able to travel farther and faster than ever before.

And so, with steam engines to do things men wanted done, progress went on and on. Later inventors, who discovered how to use electricity and gasoline, did not have to struggle as Watt did. They did not have to make tools and hammer metals by hand. For steam power was there to serve them.

James Watt saw only the beginning of all this. But he must have guessed that he was one of the great inventors of the world. Honors were heaped upon him by scientists in many lands.

The last years of Watt's life were very happy. His son turned out to be a fine and clever fellow. Young Watt and Matthew Boulton's son together ran the Boulton factory and made the steam engines there.

Since he had plenty of money, Watt built a fine house in Birmingham. When he and his wife were not traveling about, they lived there enjoying their lovely garden. The inventor had a workshop in the attic, and in it he went right on inventing new things.

His wife used to worry about his overworking, especially at night. She would say to the servant, "Go upstairs, and put out the lights, the fire, and your master!"

The British people were proud of the great inventor. In London's splendid church, Westminster Abbey, there is a monument to James Watt. The words of praise cut upon the stone declare that he was a man who helped his fellows in a mighty way.

Talking Together

1. Suppose you could have visited James Watt for just one day. On what day in his life would you have liked to visit him?

2. How many things can you name that we use today that are made by hand and not by machines?

3. Why was a newspaperman at the mine to see Watt's engine set up?

4. Each of these words has been used in the story. What do they mean? How many different sentences can you make using each of them?

| cargoes | models | cylinder | partnership |
| provisions | idler | progress | monument |

5. What different kinds of engines are used today? Where have you seen them at work?

Working Together

1. New inventions are being made all the time. Find out from your father and mother what inventions we use today that your grandparents did not have. Make a poster listing all of these newer inventions.

2. The United States Government, like the British Government, gives patents to inventors (see page 122). On your roller skates you will find the word *Patented*. How many things can you find which have been patented?

3. Make believe there had been news broadcasts on the radio when James Watt lived. Write out short news items about Watt that might have been broadcast in the day's news at different times in his life.

To Do by Yourself

1. Make a list of all the different kinds of machines mentioned in the story. Try to find every one.

2. Certain words or groups of words tell *time* because they tell *how long* something went on or *when* it happened.

   Here are some *time* words and expressions:

200 years	often	thousands of years
1705	time	spring morning
then	one day	eight years old

   Read the whole story again carefully and write down all the *time* words or expressions you can find.

3. *Geography* is a study that tells about the earth and its peoples, countries, and products. Here are *geography* words used in the story. Be ready to tell what each one is.

lowlands	harbor	America
mouth of the river	mine	Clyde
water power	canals	Glasgow
waterfall	Scotland	London
railroads	Ireland	Birmingham
earth	France	England

5 AFRICAN ADVENTURE

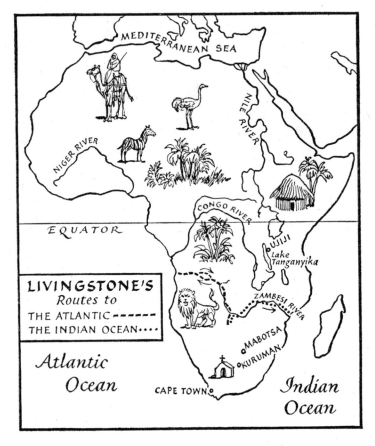

The Story of *DAVID LIVINGSTONE*

Introduction. AFRICAN ADVENTURE

WHEN young Queen Victoria came to the English throne in 1837, England was a mighty nation. Its trade was the liveliest in the world, and all around the globe it had colonies.

The newest colony was in South Africa. In those days English children were proud to point out on the big map of Africa the small spot made by this colony. Except for the old countries in North Africa along the Mediterranean, this was the only European colony which pushed inland beyond the coast. Most of the map of Africa was marked "Unexplored."

The shape and size of Africa were well known. For hundreds of years men had sailed along its coast line and visited its harbors. Trading posts thrived on both east and west coasts. The Dutch were first to settle at the Cape of Good Hope, the southern tip of the continent. In the open grassy country they started farms. Then the English won the colony in a war and set up its government in the port of Cape Town.

At that time everyone thought it would be dangerous to explore the center of Africa. Great deserts blocked the way south from Egypt and the Mediterranean. And there was no passage inland from either coast. Daring Englishmen had tried to go up both the Niger and the Congo rivers. Those who came back alive said, "The forests are dark and tangled. Rivers are too wild and rocky for travel by boat. All is wilderness without a path."

From the east coast of Africa, Arab traders managed to go some distance into the country. They scared travelers with tales of wild beasts, snakes, great rains, and savage tribes. Yet Englishmen longed to have Africa explored. Scientists wanted to learn about the rivers and mountains. Hunters were eager to get wild game. Religious people hoped to teach the savages about Christianity.

Churches in England sent missionaries to start schools and churches in the South African colony. These missionaries rejoiced when England passed a law doing away with slavery in the colony. But the Dutch farmers, called Boers, had always made slaves of the Negroes. They became so angry about the new law that they moved north and east of Cape Town to be far from English rule. The missionaries, however, knew that the Boers still kept Africans as slaves on their farms. They hoped to help in bringing this evil to an end.

The Story of
DAVID LIVINGSTONE

ON a spring evening in the year 1840, an English steamer was plowing its way through the Atlantic Ocean. The captain leaned down from the bridge high above the deck and called to the young man directly below him, "Dr. Livingstone, would you like to work out our distance from Africa now?"

The young man looked up smiling and answered, "Yes, indeed, sir! Thank you!"

With that Livingstone climbed the ladder to the captain's bridge. The captain handed him instruments for measuring distances. During the long voyage the young man had been taking lessons in making these measurements. It was hard work.

After some time Livingstone handed back the instruments, did some figures on a piece of paper, and said, "By my reckoning, captain, we are three hundred and one miles from the Cape of Good Hope. How near right am I?"

The captain chuckled. "By the reckoning I made five minutes ago, we are just three hundred and thirty miles from the African coast. For a beginner in measuring distances, doctor, you did very well."

Livingstone, looking pleased, was about to go down on deck again. But the captain stopped him. "Tell me, Dr. Livingstone, will you serve as doctor or preacher at the mission?"

"Both perhaps, sir," replied the young man. "I'll go straight up to the Kuruman mission and see what I am to do. Kuruman is about seven hundred miles north of Cape Town, isn't it?"

"Right," answered the captain, "and no way to get there except on your feet or in a supply wagon. Tell me, doctor, how did you happen to become a missionary? I'd take you to be a scientist."

For a moment David Livingstone looked down at the waves. Then he began to talk of his home in a village near Glasgow, Scotland. He said his father and mother had taught him the Bible as a little boy and had taken him to church. He had grown up wanting to do some real good in the world. Especially he longed to take knowledge of Christ to people who had never heard of Him.

Shyly the young man told the captain that when he was ten years old he had worked in a factory twelve hours a day. Even then he had studied by

himself. Later on he had gone to night school. Then slowly he had saved enough money to go to college. There he had studied to be both a missionary and a doctor, and now the Presbyterians were sending him as a paid worker to Africa.

The captain listened with interest to Livingstone's story. He liked young men who knew what they wanted to do.

"It will be a great adventure, captain," said David. "I met the head of the Kuruman mission in London, and he said that I might start a new mission in the unexplored part of Africa."

The captain gave a sharp whistle. "Do you want to be speared by savages, or eaten by cannibals, or killed by fever? Don't risk it, doctor! Stick to the safe places!"

At this Livingstone smiled into the starlight. Somehow he did not believe all the terrible tales told about "Darkest Africa." And anyway who wanted to be safe?

ALONG THE TRAIL

At last the ship docked at Cape Town. To David this town seemed like a small English city with its shops, army officers, and business people. Could this be Africa?

He waited there till the ship was ready to take him on to the next port. During the weeks of waiting he learned much about South Africa from the minister of an English church who was worried that slavery still kept on.

"We English know that the Boers keep slaves," he cried. "And yet we don't stop this dreadful practice."

Livingstone heartily agreed. "Yes, it's horrible to think of one person owning another person! Christ came to earth to set all men free—black and white alike."

Finally, the ship took him on to the next port. There missionaries helped him to get ready for the long walk to Kuruman. They hired a Negro guide who had been to a mission school and spoke English. Other Negroes were hired to carry packs, to cook, and to drive the oxen hitched to a wagon. In the wagon were supplies and blankets and David's boxes of books and clothes.

As they went along the trail David noticed everything—the palm and pepper trees, the birds with gay colors, the bright flowers. He bathed in brooks and learned to drive the oxen, even across rivers.

The guide grinned at the young man's happy face. "You like?" he asked.

"I like everything," replied David. "Tell me how to say in your language, 'I am hungry.'"

Already Livingstone had a notebook full of African words. The Negroes taught him the names of trees and animals. They told him that each tribe had a different language, but that if the white man learned the chief language he could get along. When David tried to say African words, the Negroes laughed. But when he got the sounds right, they would nod and clap their hands.

David liked to watch the big fellows walking so smoothly with packs on their heads. How wise they were in all outdoor things! Their sharp eyes found berries and roots which were good to eat. They could make a fire in two minutes and soon have water boiling for tea and for making meal into mush. At night they made tents of branches with blanket covers and spread another blanket over leafy boughs for David's bed.

Tired as he was from walking, David lay awake a long time each night. The stars had never been so close and bright. He liked to smell the woods and listen to birdcalls, the distant trumpeting of an elephant, and the grunts of small animals. "This is really Africa!" he thought with delight.

After two weeks of travel the guide said, "Not much food now. Today we shoot rhinoceros."

That afternoon they saw big gray shapes in the distance. Several rhinoceroses were standing in a pool of water. The wagon was stopped. Two Negroes went quickly and quietly ahead. Presently shots rang out. The big beasts rushed snorting through the long grass. But one of them lay dead in the pool. They all, even Livingstone, helped drag out the heavy body. That night around the campfire they boiled some of the meat in a big pot.

"It's good!" exclaimed Livingstone in surprise.

Only one thing spoiled the journey. This was the sight of slaves working on Boer farms. Once David saw a little girl trying to run away from her captor. He felt sick to think of any person forced to be a slave.

By the time the party reached Kuruman, David had learned how to travel in Africa. Now he longed to go on from this well-explored country to the unknown land farther north.

"WE COME IN PEACE"

At Kuruman lived many English ministers and teachers and their families. They had a large school for Negroes. Livingstone felt he was not needed at this mission. He wanted to reach the thousands and thousands of natives in Central Africa who had never heard of Christ nor known the decent ways of white men.

Soon he set off with supplies and Negro guides to find a place for a new mission. Livingstone paid his helpers, but not in money. What they wanted was several yards of cotton cloth for each day's work. He also took beads and cloth as gifts for the chiefs he might meet. For himself, he took clothes, books, maps, and notebooks.

North and east he traveled. The country was hilly and bare of woods. Often his party saw elephants, lions, and zebras. But as soon as the animals saw or smelled human beings, they rushed away.

The first time Livingstone reached a native village he was much excited. From a hilltop he looked down upon the grass roofs of mud huts. Some distance from the village the party halted. Then David followed the native way of being polite. He sent a guide to the chief of the tribe with a gift.

"Tell the chief that an Englishman, a 'makwain,' would like to talk with him. Say that we come in peace."

Presently the Negro guide came back with several tribesmen. Livingstone greeted them in the African language. They stared at him in wonder. Nobody in the tribe had ever before seen a white man. Shaking with fear, they set down gifts from their chief: an antelope steak and ripe melons from the village garden. They said the chief was willing to have the makwain make camp at the edge of the village.

As soon as Livingstone's men had built a campfire, the villagers stole out of huts to peek at the stranger from behind trees. They made no sound until they saw the white man use a knife and fork to cut up his meat. Then they burst out laughing. They had never seen a man use a fork before.

Next morning Livingstone was taken to the chief's hut. The chief sat on a stool of ivory, and on each side of him stood warriors with spears. The chief told his visitor about the rivers in his country and about the best vegetables for the garden.

Livingstone traveled on and on. At one village the chief grew so friendly that he wanted his visitor to tell the whole tribe about the religion of the Christians. So he called all his people together in front of his hut. David smiled to himself to be preaching to people whose only clothes were a few ornaments and feathers and scraps of cloth. But they listened as well as any well-dressed church-goers, and they loved the hymns that he sang to them. Every night, while he stayed, Livingstone held a service.

For nearly three years he wandered about the northern part of South Africa. He studied the native languages and customs and explored the land. From one tribe to another word spread about the wonderful white man who came in peace and spoke of a loving God. He could heal sick children and set broken bones better than the witch doctor. Everyone called him "The Wise One."

THE NEW MISSION

At last Livingstone decided to start his mission at a village called Mabotsa. It was several hundred miles northeast of Kuruman.

Learning this, the chief of the tribe cried, "Oh, if you stay, I shall dance. My people will make for you a garden, and you will get more sweet grass and corn than myself."

Twice Livingstone had gone back to Kuruman. The second time he brought back with him an English minister to help build mission-houses at Mabotsa. Two English hunters joined their party. They were delighted that David had made a trail to the north.

At Mabotsa the two missionaries found the whole tribe stricken with fear. "Lions come to our village!" the natives said. "They kill our cows. What shall we do?"

"Kill one lion and the rest will leave," Livingstone answered.

That night he woke with a start. For an instant he lay still. What had awakened him? Then he heard it again—a terrible roar. Lions! At once the village was astir. Cows bellowed in fright. Children screamed. Men shouted as they ran about lighting bonfires to scare the lions. Finally all grew quiet again.

Next day Livingstone took his gun and went with the warriors to hunt the lions. They found them in a thicket on a hill. The tribesmen were afraid. Twice they could have speared the lions as they ran, but not one spear was thrown. At last David saw a big lion

standing on a rock. Aiming carefully, he fired at the beast. As he reloaded his gun, he heard a shout from the others. He looked up to see the lion springing at him. Down he went with the lion on top.

The big animal shook Livingstone as a dog shakes a rat. It crushed his arm with a savage bite. Then a native fired at the animal, and with a roar the lion sprang away from David to claw the tribesman. At that moment the bullets did their work, and the animal fell dead.

Livingstone lay still. He felt weak and sleepy. Blood dripped from his arm. He opened his eyes to find a ring of frightened black faces looking down at him. "Makwain, you live?" asked the warriors.

"Yes, friends, I live," he answered and fainted.

And Livingstone did live. But he was a long time getting well. The other missionary nursed him until he

was able to return to Kuruman. Although he had a false joint put in his arm, it was never strong again.

While he was recovering he became engaged to the daughter of Kuruman's chief missionary. After they were married, Mary and David spent three years at Mabotsa. Both of them taught school, and David held religious services. When their first son, Robert, was born he became the pet of the whole tribe. Whenever they visited new places, the baby helped to make friends with the savages.

INLAND DISCOVERIES

Then another missionary took over the Mabotsa school, and the Livingstones started a mission farther north. David sent many reports about the tribes and the country to London. These were printed in both scientific and missionary papers. They stirred up great interest in England.

The Livingstones now learned that the Dutch farmers had raided several tribes in order to capture slaves. David was sick at heart. He said to Mary, "Such wicked deeds are enough to make the Negroes hate all white men. I'd like to start a mission in Central Africa far from the Boers."

From then on he seized every chance to explore. Once he went westward with a big game hunter. While his friend shot elephants and lions, David made a thrilling discovery. He found a lake that no white man had ever seen before. His report and his map of his discovery were sent to London. Men in the Royal Geographical Society were so interested that they sent Livingstone a reward of money.

The next year he and his family went on a long journey to the northwest. There were three children now. They loved riding in the wagon and watching for ostriches and zebras along the trail. The trip was hard, and the children nearly died of thirst. Finally they had to return home. But later they started again by another route and this time reached a friendly tribe who welcomed them.

On this trip Livingstone discovered that the great river of that country was the Zambesi. Explorers had only seen it near the eastern coast where it emptied into the Indian Ocean. David was thrilled and wrote the Royal Geographical Society, "The Zambesi flows half way across Central Africa to the east." This was a very important discovery.

Livingstone, however, did not get his wish to find a good place for a mission in this part of Africa. Heavy rains and mosquitoes in the river valley gave people fever. This was a bitter disappointment. But worse still was what went on among the natives. They themselves were selling Negroes captured in battle as slaves to the Arabs in exchange for cloth and guns.

David was so shocked by such deeds that he changed his whole plan of work in Africa.

A CHANGE IN PLANS

David Livingstone explained his idea to his wife as they sat one night beside the campfire. "I see now that preaching and teaching aren't going to be enough to lift up these poor savages. They need tools and cloth and hunting guns. If English merchants could find a way to trade things with the natives, the chiefs and warriors would not sell their own people into slavery. Missions are of little use so long as the slave trade goes on."

Mary looked at her husband in amazement. "You mean you are going to give up missionary work?"

"I think that it's more important at this time to open up Central Africa. My duty, as I see it, is to find a trade route to the Atlantic Ocean. Once a route is open, supplies can be sent up here. Then teachers can start schools. The natives can be taught to raise cotton and wheat. Oh, Mary, these people must be helped."

Mary said slowly, "Yes, David, I can see that exploring in Africa is really necessary. It must be done before missions can grow. But, my dear, think what such a change in your work will mean to us! You can't take the children and me with you. We shall have to part, perhaps for years."

Tears were in the eyes of both as they looked at each other. Yet these two cared more about doing what seemed right than they did about themselves. They agreed that Mary should take the children to England. There they could go to school. Then David would be free to explore Central Africa.

Their hearts were heavy as they took the long journey down to Cape Town. They wondered when they would see each other again. But Mary bravely left with the children. David watched them as they set sail. Then, left alone, he began the great work which made him famous.

First of all he went back up to the friendly tribe living near the Zambesi River. The young prince who had just become chief of the tribe soon grew to love

Livingstone as a father. Sekeletu was the young chief's name. He would say gently to David, "You have a heart. You are wise and good. I trust you."

When Sekeletu heard Livingstone's plan to find a route to the Atlantic Ocean, he offered him guides, oxen, and food. But it was hard to find a group of tribesmen ready to take the journey. They were afraid to go so far from home.

"I will bring you safely back again," David promised.

Then a number of Negroes came forward and said, "We will go with you. We trust you. You speak truth."

WESTWARD TO THE ATLANTIC

It was a terrible journey through wild country of forests, swamps, and dangerous rivers. The western tribes were not friendly. Fierce chiefs demanded huge presents for letting the party pass through their land. Livingstone thought this an outrage and would not yield.

He would say to a chief in his friendly, firm way, "Come, let us sit and talk. I shall tell you where we go and why. Our journey may bring peace and plenty to the people of Africa."

In the end he would usually be allowed to go forward freely. But sometimes he had to make an offering of an ox or some calico or one of his own shirts.

For six months they traveled through dangers of every kind. Often they nearly starved. In the rainy season they were wet for days and nights and were sick with fever. David grew so ill that he hardly had strength enough to sit on the back of his ox. Yet he would not give up. At last they reached the seacoast.

When the Negroes first saw the Atlantic Ocean, they cried, "Is this the end of the world?"

Livingstone smiled, but he, too, thought he had reached the end—the end of his dream. He had found no river possible for boats, and he knew that the trail was too rough and wild for an overland trade route.

As he tried to recover strength at the house of a kind Englishman, he wrote up notes on the journey. With carefully drawn maps he sent them to England. There scientists, geographers, and officers of the government were thrilled over this first important exploration of Central Africa.

David's friend begged him to sail for England and get well. "No, indeed," he replied. "I promised these poor faithful fellows to take them safely back home."

On the return trip it took the party nine months to reach Sekeletu's country. As they neared the main village, one guide ran ahead to take the glad news of their return.

Never was wilder rejoicing! Half the villagers rushed out to greet the party. Bonfires were lighted. Antelopes were roasted. Far into the night the men of the tribe howled their songs of joy. Again and again the Negroes said to one another, "This makwain is like a god. He can overcome all danger, and he keeps his word."

EASTWARD
TO THE INDIAN OCEAN

During the long journey Livingstone had thought out his next move. He knew now that there was no westward route from Central Africa to the Atlantic. So he must try to find an eastward route from Central Africa to the Indian Ocean. The Zambesi River might be possible for ships. He would follow it down to the Indian Ocean. Again Sekeletu helped him on his way by giving him guides and food.

Some miles down the river David saw something very strange. White columns of mist rose straight up in the air! What could they be? Presently he heard a steady roar of water. Then he knew that he was near a waterfall.

Above the falls was a small island. "You must find a boat and paddle me over there to see the falls!" David shouted to his men.

The frightened Negroes cried, "Father, it is death! The swift river will carry the boat over the falls."

Yet David got a boat and showed a few brave helpers how to paddle safely to the island. Creeping to its rocky edge, he lay on his stomach and looked over the brink. The water's roar filled his ears. He was soaked with spray. In amazement he watched the great Zambesi River—a mile wide at this point. It fell straight down hundreds of feet and then rushed into a narrow opening between tall cliffs. The rocks below flung back the water drops into those tall columns of mist. David had never seen anything so grand. He named these falls Victoria Falls in honor of England's queen.

All the way down to the coast Livingstone made friends with the different tribes. When at last he reached the Portuguese settlements, the government men greeted him in surprise. For the first time a man had crossed Africa from the Atlantic to the Indian Ocean—a distance of 2800 miles. And on foot!

Livingstone felt triumphant because he believed that the Zambesi was a possible route from the East deep into Africa. Soon perhaps England could send supplies and teachers to the savages. As he boarded a ship for home, he felt happy.

FAME

Mary was eagerly waiting for him. So were men in the government, scientists, missionaries, and news-papermen. Stories of his discoveries had been printed in the papers, and people were eager to see him. He had to go to dinners, meetings, and celebrations.

One day as he got out of a cab on a busy London street, someone cried, "There's Livingstone, the African explorer!" At once a crowd gathered, and cheers went up. People pressed around him with questions. In terror he turned and fled. Mary said, laughing, "Oh, David! You faced an African lion, but ran from a London crowd!"

Livingstone stayed in England more than a year to be with his family and write a book about his travels. He was now one of the most famous men in the world. So eager were people to learn about Africa that every copy of his book was sold before it was even printed. Money poured in upon this man who had been poor all his life. He could have lived in comfort and peace. But Africa and the Africans called him back. All he said about his fortune was, "Now I can buy a fine boat to go up the Zambesi."

In England he spoke to many groups about Africa's needs. Queen Victoria was interested and sent for him to come to her palace. As they talked, David looked around at the costly things in the big room.

"Ma'am," said he, "an African feels rich if he has a cow. When I told the natives that my chief was the Queen of England, they asked if she were rich. I always said, 'Yes, very rich.' Then, ma'am, the Negroes would ask, 'Well, how many cows does your chief own?'"

At this the Queen laughed merrily.

AGAINST SLAVE TRADE

Mary Livingstone with her youngest boy went back with David to Africa. The older children were left in school. But on the way Mary was taken ill and had to stay with her parents at Kuruman. David sailed on up the east coast of Africa to the mouth of the Zambesi River.

There disappointment awaited him. His boat was a failure. When he explored the Zambesi, he found the river too full of fierce rapids and rocks to be safe for boats. But with his usual courage he began to explore other rivers. In the year 1859 he discovered two mighty lakes.

Finally he reached a big village called Ujiji. It was on Lake Tanganyika, which another Englishman had discovered.

In this part of the country David saw men who had filed their front teeth into fine points. They looked like fierce animals. Many of the women wore iron rings fastened through the upper lip so that they could neither laugh nor eat comfortably.

Every day was exciting to the explorer. But David never stopped being a missionary. He held services wherever he went. He did not expect the natives to become Christians right away, but he hoped to touch their hearts.

He knew now for certain that the Portuguese as well as the Arabs were carrying on a big slave trade. His heart nearly burst with pity and anger, and he tried to rescue some of the captives. Only his great wish to open trails into Africa, where good things could be brought to the tribes, kept him from despair. His wife, who had come back to join him, died of a fever. Finally, in 1864, he went back to England.

He settled down with his children and began to write another book. In it he showed how the slave trade was ruining Africa. But the British government did not want trouble with Portugal and was not ready to end the evil.

Just then Livingstone learned that Abraham Lincoln had declared the Negroes free in the United States. Praying that slavery would also cease in Africa, he went back to his work there.

At once he found that things were worse than ever. Up the trails and rivers which Livingstone had opened through friendship with tribesmen, Arabs led bands of armed men. They drove hundreds of Negroes chained together down to the seacoast. Many of the Negroes died of hunger and weariness every day. David saw black bodies floating in the river. He found children dying alone in the forest.

Worst of all was the change in the Africans themselves. Greed made the chiefs ready to battle with neighboring tribes in order to sell captives for guns and cloth. Fear made helpless people unfriendly to strangers. The lovely village of Ujiji was now full of slave traders and rascals. Livingstone had to have his letters and goods sent there while he was exploring. He had to send his own letters back to the coast by messenger. But he feared that he could find no one who could be trusted.

Nevertheless, he set out with a party of helpers into unknown country west of Lake Tanganyika. Several of his hired men ran away or grew surly and mean. But two of them, Susi and Chuma, who had been at a mission school, were devoted to their leader. They nursed him when he became ill and stuck by him through danger.

Now it was hard to get food at the villages. When the tribesmen saw strangers coming, they dashed for their huts screaming, "Arabs! Arabs!" Then warriors came out with spears ready to fight. David calmed them with patient words.

"I am a peaceful makwain," he would say, "I hate slavery and look only for rivers and mountains."

162

He suffered with the Negroes over the terrible things which were happening. Arabs burned villages, tore up gardens, and drove whole tribes into hills and swamps. Because David brought a little peace to the hearts of the Africans, his very name was loved.

STANLEY TO THE RESCUE

When David's supplies gave out he had to turn back to Ujiji where he had left stores. He said to Susi and Chuma, "Boys, we've been gone a whole year. It will be good to get all the letters waiting for me."

But at Ujiji he found only one letter. And Chuma came running to say, "Master, all the stores have been stolen!"

David flung himself on the cot of his little hut. What could he do now? He had no cotton cloth to pay his helpers or buy his own food. Without stores he could not even reach the coast to sail for England.

Susi and Chuma spent days watching him anxiously. Then one morning Susi came shouting, "Master, a white man comes up the trail. Maybe he help you!"

From his porch David could hear an uproar in the village. With a long train of guides, the stranger was arriving. Was he a prince?

Suddenly Susi brought to the hut a tall, well-dressed young man. Behind him, followed by the crowd, was

a tall Negro proudly carrying an American flag.
Snatching off his sun helmet, the young man said,
"Dr. Livingstone?"

David felt his hand grasped by trembling fingers.
The stranger spoke excitedly, "Dr. Livingstone, I am
Henry M. Stanley, a newspaperman. The *New York
Herald* sent me to Africa to find you."

"What?" exclaimed Livingstone in amazement.
"How could this be?"

Stanley replied, "Perhaps you don't know that for
years no letter from you has reached England. Everyone feared that you were lost. My editor resolved to

164

spend thousands of dollars to get news of you, the most famous explorer in the world. Thank God I've found you, sir!"

David groaned, "Then that means that all my letters and reports have been lost! My stores have been stolen, too."

Then Stanley had his men open his packs. There was food of every kind, rolls of cloth, medicines, clothes—everything David had needed so much. He could only gasp, "It is magic!"

For days the two men did little but talk. Stanley reported the many world events of the past three years.

Livingstone talked of his discoveries in such an exciting way that Stanley was thrilled by the wonder of Africa. Years later he, too, became a great explorer.

AFRICA'S TRUE FRIEND

For three months Livingstone enjoyed the young American's companionship. When Stanley had to leave, he begged his new friend to go with him. But David felt that his work was not done, and the two men bade one another a sad farewell. Stanley took Livingstone's notes and maps with him. The moment he reached India he cabled the *New York Herald* that he had found Livingstone. The news flashed around the world to rejoice millions of people.

Meanwhile, far from sight or sound of his own great fame, David Livingstone went on with his work in the wilderness. Chuma and Susi stayed with him. And when a year later their great leader died of fever, the faithful boys brought his body and journals safely to an English ship.

Livingstone was buried beside kings and heroes in London's Westminster Abbey. But his real reward was the mighty effort to end the slave trade which his reports aroused in England. Through him the great continent was opened. He was the truest friend Africa ever had.

Talking Together

1. Why did Livingstone want to explore many parts of Africa instead of staying in one village?

2. Why should a New York newspaper send a reporter to search for an Englishman in Africa?

3. You cannot expect to remember all of the things that the story tells you, but you will want to remember some. Decide together what you think are the few most important ideas that you will still want to know twenty years from now.

4. The author wrote twelve titles for different parts of the Livingstone story. Can you tell why the title for each part was chosen?

5. If you could have a large copy of one of the pictures to keep, which one would you choose? Why?

Working Together

1. Choose committees of three. Have each committee select one of the sections of the story. Decide which part would be most interesting to dramatize and prepare a scene for the class.

2. On a very large piece of paper make a map of Africa. Using colored crayons, draw and label rivers; put in towns and other places mentioned in the story.

3. Bring to class the front pages of some newspapers. Study the headlines to see how important news is put in a very few words. Write some headlines about Livingstone that might have appeared in an English newspaper at different times.

167

4. Decide which new words should be added to your picture dictionary and prepare the pages.

5. Suppose that in Livingstone's time there had been newsreel cameramen. Make a list of the "shots" you would most like to see in a newsreel of his adventures.

To Do by Yourself

1. Do you know these geography words? Show how well you understand them by using each one in a sentence.

continent	inland	native customs
island	harbor	coast line
seacoast	desert	forest

2. The story uses words that you will find in many history books. Find these in the story and be ready to tell what they mean.

colony	to settle	unexplored
discovery	government	trade route

3. Make a list of all the things that Livingstone and other white men took with them to Africa. Try to decide why each kind of thing was taken.

4. At the public library ask the librarian to help you find more information about Livingstone.

6

HERO OF THE
FAR NORTH

The Story of *FRIDTJOF NANSEN*

Introduction. HERO OF THE FAR NORTH

THE Far North has never seemed so important to the people of the world as it does today. Airplanes flying between the largest cities of the world follow the short routes over the Far North. These routes are shorter than any others.

To fly such routes, an aviator must know many things. He must know about northern winds and air currents. He must also have maps showing mountain, plain, and valley. In this Polar region storms and cold are partly due to the sea currents which swirl about in a strange manner. A pilot on this northern trip has to know about these special currents and to be certain where ice stops and land begins. Today he does know all these things. For during many, many years explorers gathered knowledge about the Far North.

Hundreds of years ago the work began. The Norsemen were the first to sail in northern waters. They settled Iceland, discovered islands, and told people much about that part of the world. That helped fishermen and explorers living in northern countries. But hundreds of years passed before anyone tried to reach the North Pole. Then all at once men from many lands tried to do so. Some of these explorers were scientists who believed that it is man's task to find out everything possible about the whole earth.

Polar exploration was hard, dangerous work. Many a ship was crushed by great blocks of ice. Many a brave man lost his life. Yet others followed on. Little by little the whole north was mapped. Men found out about air and water currents and about the animals, fish, and birds living in the region. Such discoveries helped fishermen, sailors, geographers, and weathermen. Today they help our aviators.

The people of Norway always took deep interest in these discoveries. They are sons of the Vikings, and for years have sailed the ice-filled seas. The most northern coast of Norway lies at the edge of the Arctic Ocean. In that region deep snows bury the earth in winter, and the sun is not seen for months. Even in the south of Norway snows cover hills and mountains, and the lakes freeze solid. No wonder boys and girls in Norway all learn to skate and to ski.

One young Norwegian became a famous explorer. Fridtjof Nansen was his name. He was a great person who served not only his own country, but every country. His wonderful adventures were more than exciting. They helped other men learn more about this earth.

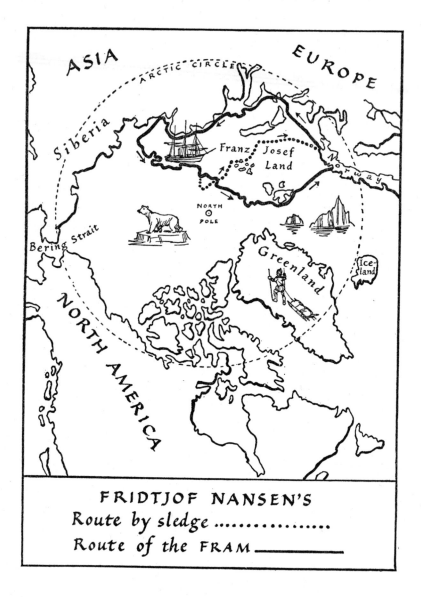

FRIDTJOF NANSEN'S
Route by sledge ....
Route of the FRAM _____

The Story of
FRIDTJOF NANSEN

OFF TO HUNT SEALS

"ICE ahead!"

From the lookout high above the deck the shout rang through the dark ship. Men came running up from below. The captain snatched up his telescope. Everybody pressed close against the rails to stare through the night. They were on a sealing ship bound for the ice fields where seals gather. They had left Norway in March, 1882. Now, seven days out of port, they were nearing their goal.

Turning to a tall young man beside him, the ship's mate asked, "See anything, Nansen?"

"Not yet," was the reply.

At that moment, everyone gave a shout. A huge cake of ice shot past the ship. Another and another followed. With a grinding sound they bumped to-gether or brushed the side of the ship. Then the shining blocks slid away into the darkness.

"Look!" cried Nansen. "What is that strange light in the north?"

The ship's mate chuckled. He was an old sealer and nothing surprised him. But this young Nansen had never been so far north before.

"You see light from the great ice fields flung up on the clouds," answered the mate. "The northern lights are beginning to play now, too."

To Fridtjof Nansen this was a magical scene. He saw glittering ice shapes floating past. He watched towers and hills of frozen water. In the distance over the ice fields, tongues of blue, rose, and silver light leaped to the sky. Ahead lay the frozen North!

Nansen was the last to leave the deck and go down to the cosy cabin. It was full of men singing as one played the banjo. They welcomed him joyfully. The young man was studying to be a scientist and had joined this sealing ship in order to study life in the Far North. In his cabin were many scientific tools. He would catch fish and cut them up for study. Every few days he lowered a thermometer into the sea to take the temperature of the water. His notebooks were filled with sketches of the big birds which flew around the ship. The other men loved to talk to him. But they wondered whether this college boy could stand the hard work of catching seals. They wondered if he could shoot straight and swim in freezing waters.

The ship was now near Jan Mayen Land. Somewhere on the ice floes not far away the seal pack gathered in early spring.

"Why do they come to the same place every year?" Nansen asked the captain.

"Well, seals don't like solid ice. They want to be able to jump into the water to fish or to escape polar bears. On broken drift ice they feel safe."

"And do ice floes always drift near Jan Mayen Land?"

"Yes," said the mate. "The polar current comes down east of Greenland, and an arm of it flows straight east, pushing broken ice with it."

Nansen said eagerly, "More ought to be known about these northern sea currents. Some of them go straight north. Where does the main polar current go when it gets to the southern tip of Greenland?"

The captain thought for a moment and then he answered, "Well, I believe that it turns west and then north up along Greenland's west coast."

HUNTING IN NORTHERN WATERS

Weeks passed before they found the seals. Then Nansen joined the hunt. He had to learn how to skin seals and bring the skins with their thick layers of blubber back to the ship. The skins made fine furs, and the blubber was boiled into a kind of oil.

Killing so many harmless seals was hateful to Nansen. But the chase was exciting. The men piled into boats and rowed quietly up as close to the ice floe as possible. Then they had to shoot the big seals straight through the head. If one was only wounded, he would flop into the water and scare the other seals into jumping into the water, too.

After his first hunt, Nansen came back with many seals. The other men were proud of him, and the captain asked, "How do you happen to be such a good shot?"

Nansen grinned. "My brother and I were brought up on a farm near Oslo. It was on the edge of a fjord with a mountain and deep forest behind it. Even as small boys we went alone into the woods for days. We lived on the fish and game we caught, built our own shelters, and slept in front of a campfire. In winter we went on skis. Skiing was as natural to us as walking."

"We had to learn to shoot or starve," continued Fridtjof, laughing. "But we only killed an animal for food. What we liked was to study animals and plants. I suppose that's why I want to be a scientist. This has been a great trip. I've found fish up here which were never before known as Arctic fish. My reports will surprise many scientists."

A few days later, Nansen was excited to see a school of whales. Most of the crew lined up and blazed away with their guns at one whale. But the huge creature calmly swam away. The men did catch sharks, however, and Fridtjof was surprised to find shark liver good to eat.

In June the ship got stuck in the ice. It could not move even an inch through the frozen channels. The captain was disgusted.

On the second morning of being icebound, Fridtjof was wakened by the mate's loud voice right in his ear, "Hurry up and turn out. There's a bear near the ship!"

In an instant the young man was pulling on his clothes. This was what he had been wishing for—a chance to hunt polar bears. By the time he had slid down the side of the ship to the ice, the bear had climbed on an icy hump to look around. Nansen took careful aim. Quickly he pulled the trigger of his gun. Bang! went the shot, right into the bear's chest. The animal roared and stumbled off. Nansen ran after it, jumping over the cracks in the ice. When he finally killed it, several men came from the ship to help drag the huge bear on deck.

"Hurrah for Nansen!" cheered the men who had been waiting and watching on the ship.

That was Fridtjof's first bear. But there were many more exciting hunts.

At last the ship began to move, drifting slowly with the big ice floe. Then one day in early July a cry came from the lookout, "Land in sight!" With a bound Nansen was on the rope ladder climbing up to the lookout. There in plain sight was the east coast of Greenland! In the bright sunlight he saw a line of mountains, rough rivers of ice called glaciers, and dark peaks between fields of snow.

When at last he came down on deck, he said to the captain, "This part of Greenland has never been explored. It would be grand to see what it is like!"

"Don't think of anything so crazy!" snorted the captain. "Put your mind on something sensible like today's chart. Our position shows we've drifted north."

"How could that be?" cried Nansen. "I thought the current here ran southwest."

"Well, young man, as you say, these currents are strange."

Nansen's last bear hunt brought two thrilling adventures in one afternoon. While chasing the first bear he fell into the water. As he was scrambling up on a slippery cake of ice he found himself face to face with the big beast. Before he could shoot, the bear jumped into the water. Nansen leaped after it, landing on a small cake of ice. As he stood there trying to

balance himself, the bear came out of the sea right in
front of him. One quick shot, and the big white bear
was dead.

From the distance the captain shouted, "I thought
you were done for that time! Go back to the ship at
once and get dry!"

Nansen started to obey. As he neared the ship he
saw three members of the crew starting off on a hunt.
He just had to join them.

This time he ran mile after mile and swam the
channels between ice floes. It took an hour to tire out
the bear and shoot it. Cold and wet, the men made
their way back to the ship with their big prize.

Now the ship began to drift faster with the ice, sometimes as fast as ten miles a day. Since there was no wind, Nansen believed it was the current that was sweeping them along. He made a chart showing just where the ship had drifted.

After twenty days the ship was freed from ice. Slowly it crawled between the floes to open water, then swiftly steamed toward Norway.

A NEW PLAN

As soon as Nansen reached home, he unloaded charts, notebooks, sketches, bearskins, and samples of fish, stones, and sea animals.

"Now the Far North is in my blood!" he told his family. "I can hardly wait to get back to it."

He had to wait six years, however. During those years he had charge of the museum at Bergen. At the same time he went on with his studies in science at the university. His work, particularly a report on whales, made him well known to other scientists. In his spare time he read everything that had been written about northern exploring. When, at last, a vacation was in sight, he was ready with a plan.

One day while visiting his home in Oslo, he asked his friend Eva Sars to go skiing with him. They climbed to the top of a mountain near the city and looked down at the snowy valley and the dark fjord.

181

Suddenly Nansen said, "Eva, next spring after I finish my studies at the university, I'm going to ski across Greenland."

"What! Fridtjof, you're simply mad!"

He laughed at her amazed face. "That's what they all say. But I've thought out a fine plan. All I need is the money. The world has to know what the center of Greenland is like."

In silence the girl looked at the tall young man. With his keen blue eyes, his great strength, and the courage in his handsome face, he looked like a Viking.

"Well, Fridtjof," she said, "you love the outdoors too much to be shut up in a museum. I hope you can have science and adventure all in one!"

182

It seemed, at first, as if his plan would fail. Men in the government and at the university said that crossing Greenland was impossible. Others had tried and failed.

"They failed," said Nansen, "because they always went the wrong way. They started from the west coast where there are villages and went east into the lonely ice fields. When anything went wrong, they had to go all the way back. My party would do just the opposite. While we are fresh and strong, we will land on the unexplored east coast and cross toward the western settlements. We'll be going toward help instead of away from it."

At last Nansen was given money for his trip and he began to get ready. Each week he spent a day and night in the mountains. He tried out sledges to find the best kind for hauling supplies. He slept in one kind of sleeping bag after another until he found the very warmest. Knowing that on the ice fields he would find no wood for a fire, he invented a special stove with an alcohol lamp. It could heat coffee and soup even in a high wind.

Meanwhile he chose the members of his party. Three were Norwegians. Two others were men from Lapland who were used to living on ice and snow. Nansen knew that these men would be able to stand the hardships of exploring Greenland.

ACROSS GREENLAND ALIVE!

In May, 1888, the explorers started from Oslo in a sealing ship. Just off the southwest coast of Greenland they lowered from the ship two small boats. These were packed with sledges, food, tools, and blankets. Nansen stared at the snowy mainland only a few miles away. Six years before he had longed to explore this land. Now he was really starting!

"Hurrah for the heroes!" yelled the ship's crew. Waving and laughing, the men took up the oars and pulled away. An hour later they could no longer see the ship. They were alone in a strange, frozen world.

Nansen said cheerfully, "Let's pull hard, boys. We're not far from shore. We'll make it soon."

He was wrong. It took them twelve days to reach the mainland. The drift ice was hard to pass and a terrible storm drove them far out of their way. Finally they reached the mainland and everyone shouted for joy. Almost as soon as they landed, Nansen began unpacking crackers, jam, and cheese. "Tonight we'll have a feast," he said.

The next morning the party followed their chosen route which lay along the mountain ridge. All the supplies were packed on sledges, and off they started. Nothing but ice and snow lay ahead. Not a plant, bird, or animal could be seen in this region.

On the first morning Nansen looked at his companions with a roar of laughter. "Do I look as queer as you do?" he asked.

He did, for all were dressed alike. They wore the thickest woolen clothes and stockings. Canvas coats with hoods were pulled over warm jackets. Dark glasses kept from their eyes the glare of sun on snow. And over their faces were tied red silk veils to keep out the wind.

Looking at one another, the men began to laugh. Certainly their friends back home would never know them in these outfits.

By day the hard work of pulling sledges kept everyone warm. At night the party halted, laid down a wooden floor all in one piece to keep out damp and cold, and set up a tent over it. On the alcohol stove they heated soup and served crackers, cheese, and canned meat. Then they crawled into sleeping bags laid side by side on the tent floor.

In the morning, Otto, a sea captain, would wake up first and shout, "Oluf, how cold is it?"

Oluf was the party's weatherman. Sometimes he would say it was warm—only twenty degrees below zero! Often he would say it was really cold—at forty-five degrees below zero! Then the men would find their hair and beards frozen. But thanks to Nansen's planning, they all kept warm and had enough to eat.

For two months the six brave men pulled themselves and their sledges westward. One sunny day a snowbird flew around them. "Look! We must be nearing the coast!" shouted Nansen.

A week later they slid down from the last ice field upon dry land. As they moved nearer the coast, the men burst into shouts. "I smell grass!" "I see a flower in bloom!" "I feel earth under my feet!"

When they reached the coast, they were still far from the nearest village. Nansen and the sea captain, Otto, put together a rough boat from the wood of the tent floor. Then they paddled to Greenland's chief village.

As they got into the harbor a native fisherman saw them. He waved a sign of welcome. Then he turned

his boat and rowed hard to shore. Racing through the village, he shouted, "It's Nansen! He's come across Greenland alive!"

All the villagers came to the harbor to cheer. Next day boats were sent for the other four explorers.

A STRANGE PLAN
TO REACH THE POLE

Nansen's party waited months for a ship to take them home. During this time, Nansen visited Eskimo villages and learned much from the natives about living in terrible cold.

Finally a ship arrived which took the party back to Norway. When the heroes landed at Oslo after a year's absence, a glorious welcome awaited them. The same people who had called Nansen a madman now praised him warmly. Scientists and explorers of many nations were eager to find out exactly what the center of Greenland was like.

Nansen was now famous. He gave talks in many countries, wrote books, and took charge of the big university museum at Oslo.

He married Eva Sars, and on a hill near the woods he built a house with a tower room where he could paint and sketch. There he worked out plans for another exploring trip; this time to the North Pole.

At last he asked the government for the money needed for the trip. At the same time he explained his beliefs. He told the men in the government of an American, who in 1879 had started for the Pole in a ship called the *Jeannette*. The ship had drifted two years in ice from Bering Strait northwest. Finally it sank off the coast of Siberia. Three years later a pair of oilskin trousers and other things from the *Jeannette* were found on the southwest coast of Greenland. The current had brought them clear around the Polar Sea, past Franz Josef Land. Then it had carried them south along the east coast of Greenland and finally around the southern cape up the west coast.

Nansen said, "This report bears out all my knowledge of the Polar current. If a pair of trousers can drift that way, a ship could do the same thing."

He planned to take a ship along the coast of Siberia, let it be frozen in ice and drift toward the Pole, and then south toward Greenland.

"It could be done with a ship so well shaped and so strong that ice couldn't crush it," explained Nansen. "With plenty of heat and food, a party could live comfortably on the ship. If the trip took three years, we'd have time to study ocean currents, winds, weather, and animal life."

Nansen's plan was talked over by scientists and explorers all over the world. Everybody respected his work, and many famous men urged him to go ahead. At last the government of Norway gave him a large sum of money, and friends added to the sum. At once Nansen began to prepare for the trip.

It took almost a year to get ready. A skilled shipbuilder in Norway worked with Nansen to make a ship stronger than any which had ever floated. It was to be shaped in such a way that it could not be crushed by ice. Nansen chose as his captain Otto, who had crossed Greenland with him. The others in the party were scientists and skilled workers. One was a good cook. Eva Sars Nansen gave her husband's ship its name, the *Fram*, which in the Norwegian language means "forward."

LIFE ON AN ICEBOUND SHIP

In the summer of 1893, the party set out. Past the coast of Finland, along the shores of Russia and Siberia steamed the *Fram*. Then it turned toward the Pole. Here and there the party stopped to hunt, fish, and study stones, plants, and birds. Once Nansen and two others hunted walrus in a rowboat. They had to be careful that no walrus jabbed a sharp tusk through the boat. The hunters shot two of the big bellowing beasts and brought them back to the ship.

"Hurrah! Fresh meat for supper!" cried the crew.

Ice floes were around the ship for weeks. Then as September drew on, the *Fram* sped north as fast as possible before the ice grew too thick.

At last came the 22nd; on that day the ice closed tight around the ship. There was great excitement on board. The engine was taken apart for greasing. The sails were packed away. A carpenter's shop was set up for making everything that might be needed.

Now the ship was being moved along by the ice floe. Every second day a man worked out the exact position of the ship by the stars. Nansen noted the depth and temperature of the ocean. Each man took a turn at keeping watch on deck.

At night the men played music and games or read books from the ship's library. One evening when they were sitting around, they heard strange noises outside. The ship trembled from prow to stern. Out on deck piled the men. At one glance Nansen and the captain cried, "It's the ice pressing against us!"

Waves and tide in the ocean under the ice heaved it up and down, cracked it, and pressed it together. Only a very strong ship shaped in just the right way could stand being squeezed so hard. Although the *Fram* shivered, it was not hurt.

Every day or so the same roaring and cracking went on. Then came a day when a huge ridge of ice was pushed toward the ship. Everyone watched anxiously.

As the ridge broke into chunks against the side of the ship without crushing it, cheers rang out. "Good old *Fram!* The *Fram* forever!"

As the ice floe carried them on, Nansen turned his mind to the ship's passengers. There were fifty-nine of them—shaggy sledge dogs, given by a Russian explorer. It was exciting sport to train these wild, strong fellows to run in harness and drag a heavy sledge.

Soon a more dangerous sport began. One day the man on watch shouted, "Bears!" There, walking straight toward the ship, were three big white polar bears. They were sniffing all the strange smells of men and dogs. They had caught the smell of something cooking in the kitchen. The big bears were so curious that even being chased and shot at did not stop their visits to the ship. They even came up on deck and several times caught one of the dogs. Nansen led exciting bear hunts over the rough, icy ways.

Life on the icebound ship was easy and jolly. But Nansen worried about the ocean currents. He found that the Arctic Ocean was often more than a mile deep. This meant that currents from Siberia had little power to push ice in such a great body of water. Nansen had counted on that current to get the ship near the Pole. The ice floe was moving, but very slowly.

A DASH FOR THE POLE

After a year and a half of drifting, Nansen decided on a daring plan. He meant to leave the ship and with one companion make a dash for the Pole on skis.

When Otto, the captain, heard this he said, "You know that if you leave the ship, you can never find it again. How will you get back to Norway?"

Nansen said promptly, "When we've gone as near the Pole as possible, we'll turn back and make for open water. Then we'll cross to Franz Josef Land. There we'll wait for a ship to take us home."

The man that Nansen chose to go with him was Johansen. He was a famous skier and knew how to tell by the sun and the stars just where a place was on the map. All the other men envied Johansen this great adventure.

For months the *Fram's* workshop was busy making all the things needed for the trip—sledges, sleeping bags, tents, skis, and two strong, light boats. These were like the Eskimo canoes called "kyaks." Even new clothes of warm wool were made. Moccasins and boots were fitted over socks, snow socks, and leggings. It was March 14th, 1895, when at last the two explorers started off.

Their sledges were packed with food, blankets, tents, tools, instruments, and two kyaks. The frisky dogs were harnessed to the sledges. Ready to go, Nansen and Johansen stood on the ice floe looking up at the *Fram*. On deck Otto and the others looked down. In each heart was one question, "Shall we ever meet again?"

A brave cheer rang out. With a crack of whips and a yell to the dogs, the two men started the sledges. They were off toward the North Pole!

What Nansen hoped for was smooth ice. If the sledges and skis could slip along easily and fast, they could reach the Pole and get back to open water while their food lasted. But he never got his wish. He found nothing but hills and valleys of very rough ice. Travel was hard and slow for men and dogs. No birds, no bears, no sign of life did they see. The air grew colder and colder. One night the thermometer froze. One morning Nansen found that even in the warm sleeping bag his fingers were badly frostbitten. After three weeks all the dogs and both men were worn out.

On April 7th, Nansen skied to a high point north of their night camp. When he came back he shook his head in despair. "No use!" he said to Johansen. "Only very rough ice lies ahead. Our food is low. The dogs can't do much more. We will have to turn back now or die!"

Johansen was as sad as his leader to give up trying to reach the Pole. But he said bravely, "At least we have come nearer the North Pole by three hundred miles than any other explorer!"

On a spot at latitude 86 degrees, 14 minutes north, they set up two flags. Then they turned their faces east. "On to Franz Josef Land!" they shouted.

THE ARCTIC WINTER

All through April the ice was fairly smooth. But May brought slush in which dogs and men sank deep. Each day was a fight for life. By June most of the dogs were dead, food was almost gone, and both Nansen and Johansen were getting weak. Wearily they pushed on. Then in July they began to find open channels in the ice floe. For the first time bears and seals came in sight. Soon the explorers had plenty of fresh meat.

At last they saw open water ahead. For a moment they were wild with joy. Then they looked sadly at each other and at their companions. It was impossible to take the dogs in the kyaks. There was nothing to do but shoot these faithful helpers. A bitter, hard task!

Terrible weeks were spent in the two kyaks. The men were always in danger from storms, from walrus, and from floating ice. They were always tired and hungry. But toward the end of August they touched land. That was wonderful! Slowly through the channels they paddled around to the west coast of Franz Josef Land.

"We don't dare to go any farther," said Nansen. "Here we must spend the winter, and it's on our heels now!"

As fast as possible they built a hut. First they dug a hole in the hard earth. Around this they built walls

of stone. The roof, held up by a big log they had found
on the beach, was made of walrus hides. Blocks of ice
were dragged in to make a chimney.

As for the door, it was the kind Eskimos use—a hole
through the snow and ice covered by a double curtain
to keep out the wind. "A grand winter palace!" cried
Nansen.

Every day they shot bears and walrus. The meat
and blubber were packed away in snow mounds for
their winter store. "Nice to have nature give us such a
handy icebox!" laughed Johansen.

Hardly was the hut finished when the bitter Arctic
night set in. Only stars, the moon, and glorious
northern lights brightened the dark earth. The two

companions cooked two meals of boiled bear meat every day. Melted snow was their only drink. They slept most of the twenty-four hours. Of course they did not have any water for washing and shaving. Both men had long hair and beards, and their faces were black with smoke and grease.

"We live like bears!" said Nansen.

"Yes, and we look like bears, too!" added Johansen.

Often the men talked of the *Fram*. Was she still holding up against the ice? Would she drift down to open water and get home safely?

Slowly the winter came to an end. One day they saw in the distance the rim of the sun. Then there was an hour of daylight. Icicles began to melt. Soon it was spring! Perhaps down on the east coast of Franz Josef Land they could get help.

RESCUE

Wearily they moved on. Weeks of adventure on land and sea followed. The sun grew warmer, and now they began to hear the songs of birds. One June morning Nansen climbed on an ice ridge above the camp they had made for the night. Suddenly he shouted to Johansen, "I hear a dog barking!"

"A dog! Here? You're crazy!" called Johansen.

Nansen threw back his head and yelled with all his might. Did he hear an answer? He began to run. Far

197

away he suddenly saw a figure moving in the snow. As he ran on, shouting, he saw the figure hurrying toward him. Presently, Nansen knew the man was an explorer he had met in London. Rushing forward, he held out his hand and cried, "It's Jackson!"

Jackson shook the hand held out to him, smiled and stared. It was plain he did not know the strange, filthy, bearded creature in ragged clothes who had suddenly come across the ice field. But when he found that this man was Nansen, he was delighted.

"Come straight to my camp," he said. "I've been on Franz Josef Land for two years."

In a short time Nansen and Johansen were welcomed by all the men in camp. It was a big settlement with every comfort. Soon Nansen and Johansen had turned into nice, clean human beings again. They thought everything was marvelous—from the hot water to the canned vegetables.

In a little more than a month, a steamer came to Franz Josef Land to bring Jackson supplies. It brought no news of the *Fram*, but was ready in a short time to take Nansen and Johansen to Norway.

HEROES OF THE NORTH

On August 13th, the ship steamed into the harbor of Vardo, one of the most northern towns in Norway. As soon as the two explorers touched foot on land, they rushed to the telegraph station and sent dozens of telegrams to friends, scientists, newspapers, and relatives. Then on to Hammerfest they went.

There Eva Nansen came to meet her husband. And soon afterward came the word they had been waiting for so eagerly. The *Fram* had safely reached Norway. It was steaming toward Tromso. So off for Tromso rushed the Nansens and Johansen. When the three reached the deck of the *Fram* where Otto and the crew waited for them, there was such joy as never was before or since. The crew danced and yelled. Everyone talked at once. Otto explained that all had gone as Nansen had planned. Slowly the current had drifted the ice floe and the ship down around the west coast of Spitsbergen. When the ice finally broke away, the engine was started, and the *Fram* steamed off to Norway.

At Tromso began the wonderful celebrations in honor of the heroes. All the way down the coast the *Fram* had to stop while whole towns turned out to welcome the crew and their leader. Hundreds of telegrams and letters came to Nansen. By the time he reached Oslo, scientists and explorers from many nations had gathered to greet him.

September 9, 1896, will never be forgotten in that city. Boats lined the fjord for miles to escort the *Fram* up to Oslo. Guns saluted. Flags waved. The wharves

were a solid mass of cheering people. They could not do enough to show Nansen and his men how proud of their work the whole nation was. Processions, ceremonies, and dinners went on for a whole week.

Nansen was now one of the most famous men in the world.

"It seems like a dream!" he kept saying. "How could I be worth all this fuss?"

No one knew better than he, however, that his exploring was very important. Explorers, scientists, and geographers were all helped by his work. Because Nansen had led the way in 1895, the American,

Robert E. Peary, was helped to reach the North Pole in 1909. And it was Nansen who made it possible for Roald Amundsen in 1911 to reach the South Pole. For he not only gave Amundsen helpful advice but loaned him the *Fram*. Moreover, Nansen's exciting books taught people all over the world about the Far North.

Although he kept on with his work in science, Fridtjof Nansen served his country whenever it needed him. After the First World War, he helped all the war prisoners to get home, and he saw that children from many lands were given clothes and food and a chance to go to school. Thousands of children looked upon him as a father.

Sometimes children came to see Nansen in the tower room of his home near Oslo. He would show them his sketches of white polar bears. He told them that these were the only bears who could live in the ice fields.

Then he would laugh and say, "But once two black bears spent a whole winter in the Arctic. I know, because I was one of them."

Talking Together

1. How did Nansen prepare for his trip across Greenland? Why was each of these preparations necessary?

2. Which do you think is more dangerous, to explore in the Far North or to explore in Africa?

3. The explorations of Livingstone and Nansen took place quite a long time ago. Tell about other explorations that you have heard of being made today or in recent years.

4. What things have you learned from the pictures that you did not learn from the words in the story?

5. Which would make a more interesting movie, the life of Nansen or the life of Livingstone?

6. Study the map on page 172. Why did Nansen leave the *Fram* and make his dash toward the North Pole by sledge? How did the *Fram* get back to Norway?

Working Together

1. After discussion by the class, try to write the story of Nansen in a few sentences on the blackboard. One way to do this would be to write two or three sentences on each of the eleven sections which would tell briefly the most important ideas in each section.

2. Make a class booklet on Nansen. Plan exactly what you want in it and decide who will do the different parts.

3. Make a chart in two columns called "How Explorations Differ." At the top of one column write *Africa* and at the top of the other *The Far North*. For Number 1 under *Africa*, list something that was true about exploration there. Opposite it, in the second column write how it was different in the Far North.

4. Make a classroom exhibit on the Far North. Collect books with pictures and books with stories. Get copies of the *National Geographic Magazine*. What could class members make for the exhibit?

To Do by Yourself

1. Find these groups of words on the pages listed and be ready to explain what they mean.

> climbing up to the lookout (p. 179)
> the Far North is in my blood (p. 181)
> called Nansen a madman (p. 187)
> it's on our heels now (p. 195)
> looked upon him as a father (p. 202)

Find another group of words, like those above. Ask some one in the class what it means.

2. If you wanted to find out all you could about ways of travel in the Far North, on which of the things listed below would you want information?

northern lights	sea animals	the *Fram*
sledges	sleeping bags	kyaks
polar bears	skis	ice floe

3. Write a title for each picture in the story.

4. Suppose you had been a reporter for a newspaper and had interviewed Nansen. What questions would you have asked him that were not answered in the story?

7 DISCOVERY!

The Story of *MARIE AND PIERRE CURIE*

Introduction. DISCOVERY!

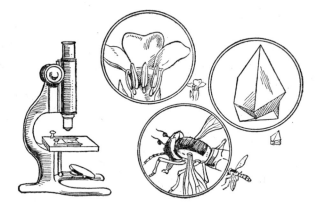

LONG, long ago wise men began asking questions about this world in which we live. "Why does a ball which is thrown up in the air always come down to earth?" "How can a big plant grow from a little seed?" Slowly the answers to such questions piled up into a great heap of knowledge. Scientists learned about stars and stones, and found out the great laws of nature.

Often something important was discovered just by watching and thinking. Sometimes scientists made daring guesses. One of them guessed that if there were no wind a heavy object and a light object dropped from a high place would fall to the ground at exactly the same speed. Then he proved that his guess was right. It often took many experiments, or tests, to prove the truth of a good guess.

Men found it easier to make discoveries after good tools were invented. Big telescopes made it possible to study the heavens and find new stars. Strong microscopes showed the wonderful forms of blossoms and crystals and tiny bugs. Men in every country shared with one another everything they learned. Thus tools grew better and so did ways of work.

The place where a scientist makes his experiments is called a laboratory. Today if you step into a laboratory, you will see a brightly lighted place, wonderfully clean and in perfect order. Work tables stretch the length of the room. There are sinks for washing test tubes and bottles in which liquids have been heated. Among the many tools are electrical instruments and scales so finely balanced that they can weigh a single grain of salt.

Scientists find out facts. Then inventors use those facts to make things. Electricity was studied in laboratories for years before it was put to work. After scientists learned how electricity acted, inventors and skilled workers were finally able to give us electric light and power. Think of a tall building with steel beams, electric elevators and lights, telephones, glass windows, and concrete floors. Many inventions and discoveries were used in putting up that building.

Sometimes it seems as if everything must have been dis-covered by this time. Yet the earth is so rich in wonders that new facts are always being found out.

This is a story about two great scientists and their great discovery. It shows how scientists work and how very much they want to find out the truth. For, like these two people in the story, many workers in science go through years of toil and hardship in order to finish their chosen task.

The Story of
MARIE and PIERRE CURIE

THE GIRL FROM POLAND

THE train from Warsaw, capital of Poland, had reached the edge of Paris. Passengers in the last car were beginning to collect their bags and boxes. Only the poorest people rode in this cold, dirty car with its hard benches. At the end of the three-day trip most of them groaned with weariness.

One passenger, however, looked fresh and eager. She was a very young woman with blond, curly hair and big gray eyes. Sitting on the edge of her bench, Marie Sklodovska gazed out of the window joyously.

An old Polish woman who sat near the girl said to her, "You look as if you thought that coming to Paris was the most exciting thing on earth."

Marie turned and nodded her head. "I've been working and saving money for this trip for years."

As she spoke a sad look came over her face. Three days ago in Warsaw she had said good-by to her widowed father, to her sister, her home, and her friends.

"Do you know people in Paris?" asked the old woman.

"Only one person," replied the girl. "She is my married sister. She and her husband are both doctors. They will help me in my work. I'm going to study at the University of Paris!"

She spoke with great pride. Marie loved to study. She had won many prizes in high school. But she could not go to college in Poland because girls were not allowed to do so. In France it was different. There anyone who could afford to study was welcome. Women could be painters or musicians. They could study medicine or law. Marie was going to study science. That was what she loved.

The meeting of the two sisters was joyful. Marie flung her arms about the tall young woman crying, "Oh, Bronya, it is good to see you! How wonderful to be in Paris at last!"

Bronya's husband was as happy as his wife to welcome Marie. He and Bronya invited their friends to meet her at their home. Most of them were Polish. Scientists and doctors came to the small apartment and talked about many interesting things. Musicians came to play. It was all delightful.

MARIE AT WORK

After a few weeks Marie said to her sister, "Bronya, dear, it is too gay here for me. I came to Paris only to study. You know I haven't much money and must make every day count. Today I rented a small attic room near the college. I'm going to move in right away."

Bronya looked very sad. But she said, "I know how you feel. You need to be all alone for real study."

From then on Marie spent her days at college and her evenings in her room studying. She would not spend money on good food. And she would not buy coal for her little stove. When she found herself shivering, she put on her coat and wrapped herself in a blanket. Her meals were always the same—bread, tea, and a bit of fruit. As days went by, she grew very thin. But every penny she saved meant that she could stay longer to study in Paris.

For the first time Marie was working in a real laboratory. As she heated things over the little gas burner and made experiments, she felt like an explorer. If she had not been too shy, she would have cried out to her fellow students, "What wonderful secrets I'm finding out!" The more she learned, the more she wanted to know.

After a year and a half she had to take a difficult examination. "I'm scared to death," she told Bronya. "Suppose I don't pass!"

Her sister only laughed. And well she might. Marie not only passed the examination, but she received the highest rank in the whole class.

After that she made a short visit to Warsaw to see her father. Luckily, while there, she got together enough money to go on with her studies. Soon she was back in Paris working harder than ever to pass a second examination.

MARIE AND PIERRE

Later that year, Marie had good news for Bronya and her husband. "I have to make a special study of steel for some men in Warsaw," she told them. "They will pay me for the work. That means I can stay on in Paris."

One of Marie's friends told her she must talk over her plan of study with a young scientist named Pierre Curie. He taught at a college and spent all his spare time in making scientific experiments. His work was so important that scientists in many countries were interested in it.

When Marie met this young man, she liked him at once. As he helped her plan her special study of steel, they saw each other often.

Very shyly Pierre said to her one afternoon, "You are not like other girls. You feel just as I do that scientific work is more important than anything else."

Marie told Bronya about her new friend. "You must meet Pierre Curie. He is very tall and slim. He has a quiet, fine face. What I think is wonderful about him is his feeling about science. To bring more knowledge into the world—proved knowledge—is what he lives for."

Pierre was finding Marie a delightful companion. Here was a young woman, pretty and full of grace, who loved to talk about hard problems in science.

Finally, after she had passed her second examination, Pierre and Marie were married.

"Look," he said on the morning of their wedding, "we have a splendid pair of horses to take us on our wedding trip."

Then he showed her two shiny new bicycles. Marie was delighted.

They packed their clothes in knapsacks and were soon on their way. Riding through woody lanes or along the sea, they almost forgot about test tubes and experiments. It was the first holiday either of them had had in years.

Nevertheless, when the trip was over, they were glad to get back to Paris and their work. They lived in a bare little apartment. But they thought it was fun because they were together.

"I'm going to learn to cook!" laughed Marie. "You're not going to starve, Pierre, just because you married a scientist."

Pierre said quickly, "Don't waste time on fancy dishes, my dear. Often I don't notice what I am eating. Cabbage soup is good enough for me."

Every evening after dinner he and his wife sat down opposite each other at a big table with their books. Pierre worked on his lesson for the next day's class and on the notes he had taken on his experiments. Marie studied for a third examination. Often they did not speak a word for hours, but they were very happy.

THE WONDERFUL X RAY

Of course the Curies shared all the scientific news that came to either one of them. One afternoon when Pierre met Marie to walk home with her he was much excited. "I've just heard about a great discovery made by a German scientist!" he cried.

This was the year 1895. Then, for the first time, the world heard of the X ray. It was produced in a special way by an electric current. The ray could not be seen, but it passed like a wave right through wood and other hard things and could make a picture on the kind of glass plate used in a camera.

Soon newspapers and magazines printed news of the X ray. One of the first pictures shown was of a man's foot inside a thick leather shoe. In the picture the shoe and flesh of the leg were dim, but the bones were so dark and clear that each one—even the smallest —could be plainly seen. Even people who knew very little about science were excited about this discovery.

Marie came laughing into the apartment one day. "Pierre," said she, "the little man who mends my shoes

216

had a photograph of that X-ray picture pinned up on the wall of his shop. He told me he thought it was wonderful."

"If only more doctors would think so!" replied her husband.

"Bronya does," said Marie. "She and her husband said at once that the X ray would help their work. If a bone is broken, the X ray will show just where the break is and how bad it is. Many doctors do not yet understand how helpful it will be to them. And, of course, many doctors are slow to take up a new idea."

Marie Curie studied the X ray carefully. After a time she learned how to make X-ray plates and gave lectures about the discovery at the university. She wanted students to understand this wonderful discovery. She wanted X-ray machines used in hospitals.

MARIE'S ADVENTURE

In the year 1897 Marie's little girl Irene was born. Those were busy days. Although she had a nurse, Marie spent hours taking care of the baby. She did the marketing and the cooking. Between times she prepared to take the highest degree given by the university. For this she had to do a special piece of scientific work; something which had not been done before. Every day she and Pierre talked over what that work should be.

One evening Pierre asked, "Marie, have you heard about uranium?"

"I've just read this report on it!" she answered. "What a strange thing it is!"

Uranium, a very rare metal, had been studied by a Frenchman the Curies knew. He found that it had a power like the X ray to send out rays strong enough to go through black paper and trace outlines on a camera plate. But it did this all by itself without any help from an electric current. Nothing like this had ever been known before. Nobody could explain how rays could come from a lifeless piece of uranium.

The man who discovered how uranium acted said to Marie, "Why don't you try to find out what causes these strange rays?"

After much thought Marie and Pierre decided that this should be her special study for the degree.

At once they started to find a place where she could work. She had to have a laboratory with plenty of space. They tried to get one at the college where Pierre taught. But the only workroom the college could give her was on the ground floor of an old building. It was dark, damp, and cold.

When Pierre came to look at the place he said, "It will do if your instruments will work all right in a room without heat. At least you have plenty of space to work."

"Well," said Marie thoughtfully, "I can use that rusty old stove. It will give off a little heat."

Neither of them worried about the danger to her health from working in such a place. They thought only of the experiment.

THE STRANGE RAYS

After a few weeks' work on a small amount of uranium, Marie told her husband of the strange way it acted.

"Nothing stops the rays from coming," she said. "Whether the room is light or dark, damp or dry makes no difference. Even if I mix uranium with another metal, the rays come right through it as strong as ever."

For months the two talked of nothing else. Even when they had dinner with Bronya and her husband, they talked about uranium. Bronya laughed at them. "I never saw such a pair!" she cried. "One would think there was nothing so important as this metal."

Marie began to ask herself, "Does any other metal give off such rays?" To answer the question she tested every single metal known in the world. Sure enough, she found another metal which gave off rays. She and Pierre were thrilled.

They said to each other, "Minerals and metals are supposed to be dead. But something active is going on in these lifeless things." Marie gave this action a name —*radioactivity*.

The rays which uranium gave off could not be seen. But they could be measured with an electrical instrument. Whenever the instrument was placed near some uranium, the rays would move a needle on the face of the instrument. When the rays were powerful, they moved the needle far over on the instrument.

As Marie used this instrument to measure earth, or ore, which contained uranium, she became puzzled. She knew there was only a small amount of uranium in the ore, yet the ore gave off strong rays.

"Such a small amount of uranium couldn't give off such strong rays," she said to Pierre one night. "I believe there is another active substance in this ore. Something new!"

Looking at her thoughtfully, Pierre replied in his gentle voice, "How could that be? Every metal, every substance on earth has been discovered and named by scientists."

Marie went back to her laboratory to prove her guess. After many more experiments she felt sure that she was right.

"I think that there is something science hasn't discovered that causes these rays," she said to her husband.

"How can you prove it?" asked Pierre. "Such a guess must be proved beyond a doubt."

"Somehow," answered Marie, "I'll have to get this substance out of the radioactive ore and see what it can do by itself. I'm certain it's there."

Pierre was not certain at all. But he had great faith in his wife's knowledge and thought there was a chance she was right. "I'll help you!" he said.

THE EXCITING SEARCH

Although Pierre went on with his teaching, he gave up all his own laboratory work. Every day, side by side in the cold room, the two scientists made experiments; Marie in her smock, Pierre in his long linen coat. Each day was happy and exciting. Had someone said to them, "I'll give you a million dollars if you'll stop this work at once," neither of the Curies would have paid any attention.

One Sunday night at supper with Bronya and her husband, Marie had special news for her sister. "Pierre and I have found that there isn't just one substance at work in uranium ore. There are two substances. The one we're sure about I have named polonium. Can you guess why?"

Bronya smiled happily. "In honor of our dear Poland, of course. What a fine idea!" she exclaimed.

The discovery of polonium surprised scientists everywhere. But the Curies knew that a greater surprise was to come. Polonium itself had strong radioactivity. But the metal left in the ore, which they had not yet found, must be many times more powerful than polonium.

"Even if we haven't seen it yet," said Marie, "let's give it a name."

"You must name it," smiled Pierre. "You guessed it was there."

In the year 1898 Marie's name for the unknown metal was first printed in a scientific paper. Radium! Nowadays that name is known in every country of the world.

One afternoon the busy pair had a visitor in their workroom. A French scientist who knew them well had come to talk about their problem.

"Do you mean to tell me," he cried in astonishment, "that what you call radium may be only a millionth part of the ore you've been using?"

"Yes," replied Pierre with a quiet smile, "yet that tiny bit gives the ore strong radioactivity."

The scientist turned to Marie. "But to prove that there is such a thing as radium you have to see it and weigh it. Can you get enough to prove your guess?"

Marie's gray eyes sparkled. "We're going to get a ton of ore from a mine in Bohemia. From that ton we ought to get a small amount of pure radium."

The visitor glanced around the gloomy room. "I wish you had a good laboratory for this heroic work."

Pierre Curie sighed. "My one hope," he said, "is for a fine modern laboratory. We shall have to do this work in a shed out in the yard."

One morning a big cart rattled up to dump the bags of ore from Bohemia into the yard. Marie was thrilled.

She seized a knife, slit one of the bags, and snatched up a handful of dark earth. "Look, Pierre," she cried, "radium is hidden in this!"

THE DISCOVERY

Radium was so well hidden that for more than three years the Curies were busy tracking it down. Marie shoveled the heavy ore into a huge kettle on the stove and stirred it for hours. She poured off the liquids and carried large jars from place to place.

Often the task seemed hopeless. Marie grew thin, and Pierre was almost sick with weariness. But they never gave up. And at last they succeeded.

Late one afternoon the two companions stood looking into a little glass tube fastened in a small rack of lead. In the bottom of the tube was a tiny amount of something that looked like a pinch of salt. All day they had put this substance through one test after another.

At last Pierre tore his eyes from the tube to look down at the small figure beside him. "Forty-five months ago you said there was a metal that science hadn't discovered. Now, here it is. We see it! We have weighed it! It is a fact! You have discovered radium!"

Softly Marie answered, "Without you it would never have become a fact."

Locking the door of the shed behind them, they walked through the noisy streets of Paris in silent joy.

After dinner, when they had put Irene to bed, Marie whispered to her husband, "Let's go back to the workroom!" With a happy nod he quickly snatched up his hat.

As they reached the dark building, Madame Curie said, "Don't light the lamp!"

They stepped into the room. There it was, their marvelous treasure. From the small glass tube bluish rays shone brightly into the darkness. The tiny bit of substance seemed alive and full of strange power. Standing before it, side by side, the Curies knew that radium was a great discovery.

Soon the whole world knew it, too. Scientists called the new substance a great and important discovery.

Scientists had believed for a long time that every thing and every being on earth is made up of tiny unseen atoms. But until radium was discovered nobody guessed that atoms could have an activity of their own. Within a grain of radium, atoms are exploding all the time to give off light, heat, and gas. Scientists now had to rewrite many of their books to explain radioactivity.

RADIUM FOR HOSPITALS

Soon it was found that radium was more than a strange metal. It could be used to help people by curing some diseases. This was thrilling to the Curies.

Just as soon as it became known that radium was useful in curing disease, doctors in many lands wanted to buy it. Therefore a number of factory owners in certain countries planned to produce radium and other metals with radioactivity from the ore containing them. But they could not do this without help from the two discoverers. The only pure radium in the world was in the old shed where the Curies worked. They were the only people in the world who knew how to get radium from uranium ore.

Letters came to them from factory owners. Large sums of money were offered them for advice and help. Businessmen believed the Curies owned this special knowledge and would expect to be paid for sharing it. In no time at all they might have been very rich.

Pierre handed his wife the first of these letters. "What do you say to this, my dear?" he asked gently.

She read it. "Why, Pierre!" she exclaimed. "We want radium to be produced for hospital use. We can't take money for our knowledge. There are no secrets in science. Discoveries belong to all the world."

He smiled happily. "Of course I knew you'd feel that way. When a scientist makes a discovery, that is his reward."

From then on both the Curies helped everyone who wished to study radium or to produce it from ore.

GREAT HONORS

In the midst of all the excitement over radium Madame Curie had to take the examination for her degree. Before a group of scientists at the University of Paris she had to answer questions about her work. Bronya, who now lived in Poland, rushed back to Paris for the great event.

"Marie," she cried, "you must come with me to buy a new dress. You can't appear in that old black thing."

Marie looked sad, for she liked her old clothes best. But she went very meekly to buy a new dress.

It was a great day at the university. The room was packed with scientists and famous people, with friends of the Curies and a number of newspapermen. There was a murmur of excitement when Marie came into the room. She looked young and lovely. Quietly she talked about the work that she and her husband had been doing in the last four years. Patiently she answered questions. A stranger would never have guessed that this modest young woman had made one of the great discoveries of our times.

After that June day in 1903, fame came swiftly to the Curies. At first only scientists honored them. They were invited to London where Pierre told English scientists about radium. Later in the year a letter from Sweden came to Pierre. When he opened it he gasped in surprise.

Some years before this, a very rich man in Sweden named Nobel had worked out a wonderful plan. He gave a huge sum of money to be used to reward those who do most for peace and for the good of the human race. Every year a group of wise men in Sweden choose from any and every country the persons worthy of this reward. The letter Pierre Curie opened said that he and Madame Curie and the scientist who had discovered the strange rays in uranium had been chosen to share the Nobel prize in science.

Marie read the letter in amazement. "Pierre, can you believe it? What an honor! And this means that we will receive about twenty thousand dollars."

Everyone all over the world is interested in those who receive the Nobel prize. Every newspaper, even in small towns, prints their names. Overnight the Curies became famous in every country around the globe. Newspapermen came to the old shed to take pictures of the place where radium had been discovered. Photographers found the small house which they had rented in a quiet part of Paris and took pictures of it. They also took pictures of Irene and of

the little garden where Marie raised flowers. Visitors came to see them at the workroom and at the house. Magazine editors begged them to write articles.

Some people would have liked all this excitement. But Pierre and Marie hated it. They loved quiet. They were too shy to enjoy many people. Most of all, they disliked having to stop their experiments in order to see strangers and to have their photographs taken.

"How can we get on with our work in all this hubbub?" moaned Pierre.

But they both had to laugh over one newspaper story which told about their black and white cat. "Even our poor pussy is not left in peace!" they said.

"Let's get away for a bit!" said Pierre. "Let's take our bicycles and go down by the sea!"

They did this every now and then. Dressed in their old clothes, they spent days in a fisherman's cottage. Nobody dreamed that these simple people were the famous Curies. They liked that very much. It was about this time that a second daughter was born. They named her Eve.

At last the University of Paris honored Pierre Curie by making him a professor. He had hoped that he could have a modern laboratory in which to work. But he was only given two workrooms which he had to fit out as best he could. This was a disappointment. However, he loved his work.

One evening the Curies were invited to dinner by the president of France. Pierre looked at his wife in her black evening dress trimmed with a bit of lace. "You look lovely," he said admiringly. "What a pity we have no time for enjoyment!"

Marie burst out laughing. "You know we enjoy our work more than anything else in the world, Pierre."

Suddenly in April, 1906, a cruel and terrible thing happened. Pierre Curie was knocked down by a wagon drawn by two big horses and killed. The world lost a great scientist, and Marie lost her happiness. Only her love of Irene and little Eve, and her devotion to science made life bearable to her without Pierre.

Madame Curie was asked by the University of Paris to teach in her husband's place. This was a great honor, for no woman had ever taught there before. For Pierre's sake she accepted the task. She also directed work in the laboratory where several young scientists now helped her. Still, she found time to be with her two children a great deal. She was too sad to play or laugh with them, but they loved her and she took joy in them.

In the next eight years many countries gave honors to Madame Curie, and again she received the Nobel prize. Best of all, a fine laboratory was being built for her in Paris. It was to have everything that she and Pierre had always needed for their work.

"I'm even going to have a garden," she said to Eve and Irene. "I'm planting trees in it."

WAR WORK

In July, 1914, the building was finished. Everything was ready. Marie and her helpers were happy and excited. And then the First World War broke out.

Swiftly the German armies drew near Paris. "Will they capture the city?" everybody asked in despair. All the young men who had been working with Madame Curie rushed off to defend the country. No more experiments could be made. Marie wasted no time being sad that her work was stopped. First she

took her radium to a safe place. Then she put her mind on the soldiers. Already trainloads of wounded were being brought to Paris.

Marie said to one of her friends, "We have good doctors and nurses to care for the wounded on the battlefield and in hospitals. But one thing they do not have at the front is the X ray! And they must have it!"

She was one of the few people who understood that, because the X ray takes a picture through flesh and bone, it can show exactly where a bullet lies. Through these magic eyes, the doctor can see where to use his instruments for taking out the bullet.

Marie wrote to her daughters, who were in a safe place in the country, "My war job is to get an X-ray service started."

First she got together all the students who had been trained to use the X ray. Then she trained older people to use it. She urged that machines be made in a hurry. She asked rich women to give money to set up the machines in automobiles which could be driven straight to the edge of the battlefields. At last she had twenty cars ready. Soldiers called them "Little Curies."

She herself took the first of these cars to a field hospital. There she showed the overworked doctors what a wonderful help the X ray was. When a wounded man was brought in on a stretcher and placed on the special X-ray table, Marie would say, "This will not hurt. It's just going to take a picture."

Doctors soon learned how quickly they could find out where a bullet was in a man's body by looking at the X-ray photograph. Then they began to ask for

234

X-ray rooms in all their hospitals. Madame Curie helped get 200 of these rooms ready. More than a million soldiers were X-rayed by the machines she set up.

Marie Curie used to sleep on the floor, eat anything that happened to be in camp, and work eighteen hours a day. This small, thin woman did not tremble at the sound of guns and bombs. She was upset only if something stopped her work.

Once as her helper drove the car along a road torn up by cannon shells, a tire blew out. Madame Curie was flung from her seat into the back of the car. As she landed, a big case of glass plates for X-ray pictures fell on top of her.

Her helper cried out in a frightened voice, "Madame! Madame! Are you dead?"

Laughing, she answered, "Would you believe it if I said 'Yes, I am'? Hurry up and find out if many plates are broken. That's more important."

A GREAT WOMAN

As soon as the war was over Marie Curie opened the new laboratory in Paris. Students from all over the world came to work with her. Every morning she went from one of their experiments to another and helped each person with his work. The young men and women thought of her only as a teacher and scientist. They forgot that this quiet woman with sad gray eyes was one of the most famous people in the world.

One day an American woman came to see Marie. She was the head of a large magazine and had printed many stories about Madame Curie. As they talked together the American found out that the discoverer of radium had none of her own. The one tube in the laboratory was used only to give other metals radio-activity for use in hospitals.

"I cannot buy any radium," explained Madame Curie. "It costs too much." Indeed, a tiny bit of radium costs $100,000.

The visitor said warmly, "You must have your own radium to work with. American women who are interested in your work will give it to you, I know."

This was true. In less than a year the money was raised and the radium bought. Then Madame Curie and her two daughters were invited to the United States to receive the gift. Marie was too shy to want to go. But she was so grateful to generous Americans that she accepted the invitation. In May, 1921, she landed in New York with Irene and Eve.

Her young daughter, Eve, had not known that her mother was famous. Madame Curie had never talked about her honors. The girl's eyes grew round as she saw the flowers stacked in Madame Curie's hotel room. She looked on with pride as newspapermen took pictures of her mother. Eve was amazed to see thousands of people gathered in the streets to catch a glimpse of her mother.

Madame Curie grew ill with the strain of meetings, dinners, and receptions. But she was grateful because Americans seemed to love her. In Washington, D.C., the President gave her the radium. She received honors at many universities and was taken by special train to see the Grand Canyon in Arizona. Her two daughters thought America was wonderful and had a very good time.

After this visit to the United States, Madame Curie did not stay hidden in her laboratory. She traveled to many countries and received many honors. What she loved best, however, aside from work in science, was a simple place on the seashore where a few friends swam and boated together.

Her great pride was in her children. Irene became a famous scientist. Eve became a musician and writer.

The discoverer of radium was not only the first great woman scientist who ever lived. She was a great woman in every way. No one ever gave more to work, friends, and family. No one was ever freer of the temptation to make money. This Polish woman who spent most of her life in France did not belong to any one country. Marie Curie served all human beings. She belongs to the whole world.

Talking Together

1. Why did Marie want to leave her native land of Poland to study in Paris?

2. Why would not Marie and Pierre Curie accept money for their discovery? Would scientists today feel the same about their own discoveries?

3. Read again the very last sentence on page 238. What does it mean?

4. Of all the stories you have read in this book, which have you most enjoyed? Can you give good reasons for your choice?

Working Together

1. Here are a number of things that different class committees could do for the whole class.

   a. Make arrangements with someone in the high school laboratory to show the class how a microscope is used.

   b. Make a poster with a list of sciences, the titles of scientists, and what they do. For example: astronomy—astronomer—study the sun, moon, planets, and stars.

   c. Borrow X-ray pictures from doctors. Perhaps a doctor might show a group of pupils how he takes these pictures.

   d. Collect pictures taken through a microscope, such as pictures of snowflakes.

   e. Arrange a display on a bulletin board of famous women today. Use pictures and descriptions of what they are doing.

2. If you watch newspapers and magazines (even the advertisements) you will find pictures and information about *laboratories*. Make a bulletin board display on laboratories.

3. Make a table exhibit of instruments which give you information by means of a moving needle. There would be a barometer, a thermometer, and a compass. Are there others?

4. Talk with people outside of school. Tell them what you have learned about the discoveries of the Curies. Ask them to tell you about discoveries of other scientists made in the last few years.

To Do by Yourself

1. Here are some words used in science found in your story. Do you understand them well enough to tell some one else what they mean?

gas burner	X ray	discovery
test tubes	instruments	radium
experiments	radioactivity	laboratory

2. Locate the places mentioned in the story on a map or globe.

3. Do the pictures in the story tell you anything that the words of the story do not tell?

4. Read the story of the Curies in a children's encyclopedia. What additional things does the encyclopedia tell you about them?

8 FREE SPIRIT OF CHINA

SUN YAT–SEN, China's Hero

Introduction. FREE SPIRIT OF CHINA

CHINA is a large and very old country. For a long time the Chinese people lived by themselves. They worshiped their old gods in fine temples. They had great scholars and poets. They liked their own ways of living and doing things. So the Chinese people did everything they could to keep other people out of their country.

A hundred years ago only a few outsiders knew China. Most of its visitors were traders. But a number of men from other countries came to stay in China. They were sent by churches to teach the Chinese about the Christian religion and to start schools. This work went slowly, for most of the Chinese did not trust other peoples.

Very few Chinese knew much about the people in different parts of their country. For even as late as the year 1870, there were no railroads to make travel easy. The Chinese could travel only up and down the wide rivers in small sailboats called junks or ride in oxcarts from one village to another.

Besides the hardships of travel, there were other reasons why the Chinese did not know one another well. In different parts of China the spoken language was different. When people from the North met people from the South they could not understand one another. There were no newspapers or magazines. Very few of the millions of poor farmers and workmen could read. They knew only the tiny part of China where they lived.

For thousands of years China was ruled by emperors and empresses. At first the people had good and wise rulers of their own. Then they were conquered by a savage tribe from Manchuria called the Manchus. The Chinese had always looked down on this tribe because it had no great artists or scholars or poets. So they were very unhappy when the Manchus began to rule them.

These Manchu emperors lived in the great walled city of Peking. Most of them were tyrants who cared little about the welfare of the people. They sent troops into every state and town to make the people obey their rules.

Only a few Chinese boys were educated. They were the sons of rich men and princes, and boys who were going into business. Nobody was taught the new ways of doing things.

Traders from other countries were eager to sell tools and machines to the people of China. But the Manchu leaders made it hard for them to do business in China and demanded much money from them. Then there were small wars between China and the countries which came to trade with her. China lost the battles, and the Manchus had to let traders come into the country and bring their ships up the big rivers.

About that time the Manchus began to have trouble with the Chinese themselves. People hated the way they were treated. Police were always spying, and often a man was beheaded for some little fault or just because he complained. At last a large number of people rose up against the troops of the Manchus. Their guns were not as good as the ones which the Manchus had, but they fought like tigers. Millions of people were killed before the revolt was put down.

Everywhere in China young men were unhappy. They were sure they could never get ahead in their own country. Some went to cities in Europe. Many sailed across the Pacific to the United States or to the island of Hawaii. These young men sent back word to friends that life in China must change. Many educated people also began to wish they had a chance to govern themselves. They longed for a leader to show them the way.

SUN YAT-SEN

China's Hero

ATTACK ON THE OLD GODS

IT was early afternoon. The little village in South
China seemed asleep. No one was on the narrow,
dusty path winding between the scattered houses. All
the farmers were in the rice fields, and the women
were tending to their cooking and sewing.

Suddenly from the doorway of a small house slipped
a dark-eyed youth. He looked eagerly around. All the
houses were like his own, built of mud blocks and
roofed with woven rice-straw. In the distance the
boy saw a tall, slender figure and waved his hand.

A few minutes later the two boys met. They greeted each other in the Chinese way, speaking the last name first. "Good day, Sun Tai-cheong!" "Good day, Lu Ho-tung!"

These boys had been friends from childhood. But until a few weeks before they had not met in several years. Ho-tung worked as bookkeeper in a big city. Tai-cheong had been living with his brother in Hawaii. Since they had met again the two friends had talked by the hour. Ho-tung had talked a great deal about China. He believed that many things should be changed. Tai-cheong listened carefully to all his friend said. He hated the dull life in the village and was ready to think that everything was wrong.

Ho-tung looked anxiously at his companion. "Tai-cheong, are you truly going to do this rash thing today?"

"Yes," replied the youth, and he looked serious. "I must show my parents and the villagers that somebody is not afraid of the old gods. Often you and I have said how stupid it is to think that a statue of wood can cure sickness or bring rain. The old religion teaches nothing to help our people."

He spoke in a low tone. With his hand on Ho-tung's sleeve he drew him toward the temple which stood a little way from the houses. Meanwhile he went on talking.

"When I learned about the Christian religion in Hawaii, I began to hate these old temple gods."

His friend nodded. "I know. The Christian religion is the only one for me, too. I am sorry that your family will not let you be baptized."

"Ah!" groaned Tai-cheong. "I'll never forget how angry my brother was when I told him I wanted to become a Christian. He sent me straight home from Hawaii."

"And now," said Ho-tung sadly, "you see how poor and ignorant our people are. Each man wants to do just as his grandfather did and make no change for the better. And the Manchus keep everybody from making any progress."

"So do the old gods!" cried Tai-cheong. "Today I shall show that they ought to be destroyed and that I, for one, am not afraid of them."

The two youths entered the temple. They stood silent a moment as they looked around. The place was dusty and dirty. Spider webs were everywhere. In the dim light the painted faces of the gods seemed to stare angrily. Ho-tung stayed near the door. But Tai-cheong walked swiftly to the nearest statue and broke off its lifted finger. He scratched the paint from the next statue and took away the shining sword from the largest god. When he had spoiled every statue, he hurried out of the temple with his friend.

By night all the villagers knew what had happened. They were angry and frightened. "The gods will blame all of us who live in this village. They will punish us!" they cried. "Who did this evil thing?"

The following morning Tai-cheong's father said to him, "You were seen going to the temple yesterday. People say you spoiled the gods. Is this true?"

"Yes, honorable father, it is true," said Tai-cheong firmly. "The old gods must go. If our people would only become Christians they would have new strength."

The Suns were much upset. The mother wept. The father grew angry. They had to show the villagers that they were ashamed of their son's act. They thought that if they punished him, the gods would not punish the people of the village.

"You must leave the village this very day," said Sun. "Now you will have to make your own way in the world. To get a good job you must study the old Chinese writings. Go to Canton. You can find a teacher there."

Tai-cheong bowed his head. He did not want to study the old writings, and he was sorry to hurt his parents. But his heart leaped for joy at the thought of leaving the village and starting a new life.

TO THE BIG CITY

With a small bundle of clothes and some money tied in the folds of his thick sash, Tai-cheong walked across the fields. Not far away was the great river which ran to the big trading city of Canton. By night he was on a junk sailing down the river.

Early next morning he stood in the prow of the boat watching the sailors tie up to a wharf. He was amazed to see all the hundreds of junks and ships crowding Pearl River. Presently he stepped off the boat, crossed the wharf, and entered the street. He was thrilled to be in the city of Canton.

Instantly he was caught up in the noise and stir of the city. Merchants were opening their shops. Working men were pushing carts and wheelbarrows heaped high with goods. Cooks at little stoves on wagons were selling bowls of hot rice and fish. Everyone was talking or shouting.

"How can I get used to such a big city?" thought Tai-cheong.

After he found a place to stay, the boy took a long walk through the narrow, crooked streets. At last he saw a group of white houses behind a brick wall. Near the gate was a sign written both in Chinese and in English saying this was the Christian Mission of the Church of England. Tai-cheong felt he must find out about this mission. The gate stood open, and the gatekeeper was not looking his way. Holding his breath, Tai-cheong slipped in.

At that moment the door of the largest building opened. Out came a tall Englishman dressed in a white linen suit. With a bound the boy reached his side. "Good day, sir!" he said in English.

In surprise the man looked around. There stood Tai-cheong in wide, blue cotton trousers and a blue tunic. His hair was braided in a long, thick queue. He looked just like any other Chinese youth. But he was speaking English! And there was something in his dark eyes and in his shy smile that interested the Englishman.

"Well!" exclaimed the man after his long look. "Come into my office and tell me why you came here and where you learned to speak English. I am a doctor and have a small hospital at this mission."

In a few minutes Tai-cheong was telling the doctor about himself. He said that his father wanted him to study only the old Chinese writings. Then he explained that what he himself really wanted was to learn useful things in the English way.

As he told the doctor of the English school in Hawaii, Tai-cheong said proudly, "The king and queen of Hawaii gave me a prize in English grammar."

The doctor looked pleased. "It is good that you are not afraid of the English. Here in Canton people have often thrown stones at me and at my hospital. They do not like strangers from another country."

Then the doctor told Tai-cheong about a school called Queen's College which taught lessons in both Chinese and English. It was in Hong Kong, the island-city which the English had settled. Tai-cheong was delighted to hear this and made up his mind to go there. Thanking the doctor, he hurried back to his room.

TAI-CHEONG, THE STUDENT

That night he wrote a letter to one of his brothers who lived in another state. He begged his help in going to school.

Soon the brother sent him money, and Tai-cheong took a boat down Pearl River to the sea. In the harbor were big steamships loading tea and rice and silks. Looking up at the steep hills on the island of Hong Kong, Tai-cheong felt happy and excited.

He stayed at the school for three years. Twice he went home for a short stay. The first time was for the funeral of his father, who had died suddenly. Later he went back to marry the girl his family had chosen for him. She lived with her husband's mother and saw little of Tai-cheong for years.

Tai-cheong studied hard at school. As soon as he finished, he went back to Canton and called on the doctor at the English mission.

The doctor was glad to see him. "How would you like to have a job at my hospital?" he asked. "You could come to my classes and learn about medicine."

Tai-cheong took the job at once. He liked the doctor's classes and also the bright young men who came to them. One day as he entered the classroom he had a wonderful surprise. Who should be at the door but his old friend Lu Ho-tung!

After a warm greeting Tai-cheong asked Ho-tung why he had come to the hospital. His friend answered, "Whenever I have a vacation from my job I try to meet young men in different cities who might help save our country. I am more sure all the time that the Manchus must be overthrown."

In the next weeks Tai-cheong learned much from his friend. For the first time he heard there were many secret societies in the southern cities. He was told that the members of these societies were planning to free

China from the Manchu tyrants. As Ho-tung left to return to his job, Tai-cheong said earnestly, "If I could only start now to help you and my country! But first I must decide how I can make my living."

He stayed on at the hospital for a year. Then, one day, the doctor called him into the office. "You have done well here, Sun Tai-cheong," said he. "I think you would be a good doctor. A new medical school is going to open in Hong Kong. A very good English doctor named Dr. Cantlie is to be the head of it. Wouldn't you like to study there?"

Tai-cheong was proud that the doctor wanted him to study there. As soon as the school opened he entered it. In a short time Dr. Cantlie and his wife became his firm friends. But he worked so hard that he seldom got home to his wife. This was sad, for now he had a little son and was very proud of him.

By this time Tai-cheong had been baptized as a Christian and went to the English church. He wished more Chinese were Christians. It made him sad to see how backward his people were.

"English ways of working seem so sensible!" he told Dr. Cantlie. "You are always finding better cures and medicines. You have fine tools, and you keep everything so clean. Chinese people try to get cured of illness by praying to a wooden statue of a god or buying useless stuff from merchants."

Dr. Cantlie nodded. "Yes, there is much to be done for China. Educated men like you must help her."

THE NEW NAME

One day, eight years after his father had sent him to Canton, Tai-cheong went to see his family. As he entered the house, he greeted his mother with great respect. Then his wife bowed before him and asked, "Honorable husband, what is your news?"

"It is good news," he answered as he took his little son into his arms. "I have graduated from Dr. Cantlie's medical school at Hong Kong. I am now a doctor. And I have taken a grown-up name. No longer am I Sun Tai-cheong. Now I am Sun Yat-sen!"

His wife and mother stared at him. They both understood what the new name meant. "Yat" means "free," and "sen" means "spirit." By this name the young doctor was telling people that he was a free spirit and would go his own way in life. This was in 1892, and Sun Yat-sen was twenty-six years old.

THE JOURNEY NORTH

Soon the young doctor started to work in a coast town across the bay from Hong Kong. But as he treated sick people his mind often went back to his friend Lu. Lu was giving all his money and spare time to help free China. How and when should he himself start to do the same thing?

Meanwhile he met many young men who felt as Lu did. They too believed that the first thing to do was to stir up a revolt. How else could the Manchus be stopped? How else could they stop the wicked things which the Manchu judges did to men who could not pay them? Was there any other way to prevent the government men from spending the tax money on themselves?

As he heard one story after another, Sun Yat-sen began to feel that his own business was much less important than the work he must do for his country.

One day he said to his friends in the town, "If things are as bad in China as you say, then I must try to help. I will go to a city and watch things with my own eyes and decide what to do."

Since he knew Canton best, he went there to live. There he soon gathered about him a number of young men. Sun said to them, "Let us form a society which will do some real good. Then the Manchus will not spy on us, and in secret we'll plan a revolt."

Everyone agreed. They called their group the Educational Society. They tried to find out just what the Chinese needed for a better life. It was not long before Lu Ho-tung visited the group. Sun Yat-sen was delighted to have him there.

Lu said to the others, "There is one man high up in the Manchu government who cares about the good of China. He is starting a school in the city of Tientsin. Let us draw up a list of things which ought to be done. Sun Yat-sen and I will take it to him, and perhaps he will help us."

The Educational Society made out the list. They asked for schools to be started in villages and small cities. They asked that good machines be bought for farmers, and that farm boys be taught new ways of doing things. Then Lu and Sun started for Tientsin. This was a city on the northern coast not far from Peking, the capital.

They made the long journey partly on foot and partly by junks sailing up along the coast. After weeks

of travel they reached Tientsin. But when they went to the house where the Manchu leader was staying, they were met by frowning government men.

"Off with you!" snarled one. "Our leader wants nothing to do with people like you."

As the two young men walked down the street, Lu was pale with anger. "One good Manchu is no help," said he, "if we cannot talk to him. These men who work under him are too afraid of anything new."

"Let's go on to Peking," said Sun. "I've never seen the capital, and perhaps we could give our list to someone in the palace."

Lu agreed, and they took a junk up the river to the great city.

On that first morning in Peking, the city seemed wonderful. The temples were beautiful. So were the gates in the thick walls. In shops, they saw fine things to eat and wear. A gay wedding procession filled one narrow street. But before the day was over the two young men hated the city. They were not allowed even to see the Emperor's beautiful gardens, let alone speak to anybody in the palace. Whenever they asked questions people either laughed or shook their heads. For the language of the South was strange to them.

"Let us leave this city quickly," cried Sun Yat-sen. "These men of the North act like the Manchus."

Everywhere on the journey back to Canton, Lu and Sun saw how backward China was. There were no good roads. Houses of villagers and farmers were nothing but dirty huts. Women and little children were working hard in the bean fields, and the men were threshing rice by hand. More than ever the travelers felt that the people of China could not be helped until the Manchu government was overthrown.

A NARROW ESCAPE

When the young men reached Canton they told their story to the members of the Educational Society. All agreed it was time that the people of China had some part in their government. Lu said the hour had come to act.

"Here in the South, in Canton, we can start a revolt!" he cried. "Thousands all over the state will join in."

"And then," added Sun eagerly, "other cities will surely follow."

All the members were hopeful. Each one had the names of a hundred people who would help the revolt. Lu gave the money to buy guns. In secret they stored them in the room where the society met.

One night as they were holding a meeting, a member of the group rushed in. "We are in danger," he cried. "Spies have told the police that we have guns. This room will be searched. Let us flee!"

As fast as possible each man tried to find a hiding place. Lu helped Sun Yat-sen get on a junk that was going to Hong Kong. Sun begged his friend to go with him. But Lu said, "No, it is safer for you to go alone. I'm sure I'll not be caught."

At Hong Kong, Sun found a friend who was glad to keep him. But in a few days terrible news came from Canton.

Many members of the Educational Society were in prison, and Lu had been put to death. This was the greatest sorrow Sun Yat-sen had ever had.

"They are searching everywhere for you, Sun Yat-sen," his friends said to him. "You must leave China at once. Go to your brother in Hawaii!"

Sun agreed that this was the wise thing to do. But he knew that if he tried to get on a steamboat he would be captured. How could he fool the police? At last he thought of a way.

When he was ready, he sent word to his friends. As they came to say good-by, they looked at him in astonishment. For they saw a man in a business suit with short, dark hair and a dark mustache.

"Are you really Sun Yat-sen?" they asked.

"Yes," he laughed, "but I don't feel like myself. I never grew a mustache before, and I feel strange without my queue. Now I am a Japanese business-man, and I shall reach Hawaii safely. I shall never give up working for the good of China."

In Hawaii Sun found his mother, his wife, and his little son. They, also, had had to escape, because they were related to Sun Yat-sen. Sun feared his elder brother would be angry. But he was warmly welcomed.

"I too believe the Manchus must be overthrown," said the brother. "Go ahead with your plans. I will help you all I can."

Sun Yat-sen had decided that Chinese all over the world should join together and form a Party of the People. When the Party became strong enough, it would revolt against the Manchus. Then it would set up a republic with leaders chosen by the people. Many Chinese living in Hawaii joined at once and brought many of their friends to Dr. Sun's meetings. Soon they raised a large sum of money for his work.

"Go to the United States!" they begged him. "Tell the Chinese there about your plans!"

Following the advice of his friends, Dr. Sun went first to San Francisco. There he held many large meetings. He planned to go to Chicago and New York. But all at once he received bad news. The Manchu leader who had an office in Washington, D.C., was planning to kidnap him and send him back to China to be punished by death. Sun Yat-sen lost no time in taking a ship for England.

All the way across the ocean he was cheered by one thought. His old teacher of Hong Kong was now living in London. The moment he reached the great English city he went to see Dr. and Mrs. Cantlie and received a warm welcome from them.

"You must stay with us!" they both said. They were much interested to hear his plans for starting a party to work for a republic.

"I shall visit all the Chinese in London," said Sun, "and ask them to join with us."

KIDNAPED

One day two Chinese stopped Sun on the street and began to talk. Sun said politely that he was in a hurry, but they walked on with him. Just as they passed a tall, narrow house, the two men pushed him toward the entrance. Another man ran down the steps and seized him. As he was shoved inside the door, he suddenly remembered the house. It was the London office of the Manchu government.

His heart turned upside down. He had been kidnaped! He would be sent back to China to be killed! A few moments later he was locked in a small room on the top floor.

"If I could only get word to Dr. Cantlie," he thought, "he would rescue me!"

Sun wrote many notes to the doctor. Then he wrapped each note around a coin to keep it from blowing away and dropped them all out the window.

The next day an English servant came into the room. Without saying a word, he began to nail the windows tight so that they could not be opened. Then the prisoner knew that his kidnapers had found the notes.

In despair he pleaded with the servant. "Won't you help me? You, an Englishman, cannot know how cruel the Chinese leaders are. They will send me to China and put me to death. You can save me. Please take a message to my friend Dr. Cantlie. Look, here is his address. If you are a Christian, do this for me, I beg you!"

Although the servant made no reply, he took the paper with the address. Would he deliver the message? If not, all would be lost.

For two days the prisoner walked up and down, and prayed that help might come. On the third morning he saw from the window a group of London policemen standing around the house. He saw also a crowd of people staring up at his window. What did this mean?

All day he watched and waited. All night he lay awake hoping and fearing. At dawn he was up and dressed. Hours later he heard a key turn in the lock.

What now? The door opened, and he saw a London policeman; behind him was Dr. Cantlie! With great joy he clasped Dr. Cantlie's hand.

"You are free, Sun Yat-sen," said the doctor. "You are coming home with me now."

Trembling with relief, the young man walked out of the house with his friend.

Then he learned what had happened. The English servant's wife had taken a note to Dr. Cantlie telling him about Sun Yat-sen. Next morning the doctor had hurried to the chief of the London police. But the chief had been afraid to do anything to anger the Chinese Government. At last Dr. Cantlie had reached the head of the English Government, and there found a man who would act at once. The man had told the Chinese leaders they must free their prisoner. He had also sent police to see that Dr. Sun was not dragged off in the night. In the end the Manchus had been forced to give up their prisoner.

By this time the story of the kidnaping and rescue had been printed in a London newspaper. Then it was copied in many papers around the world. Sun Yat-sen had become a hero—above all to people of his own country. Wherever Chinese lived, whether it was London, Paris, Hawaii, New York, or Canton, they knew of Sun Yat-sen and his plan to make China a republic. They wanted to help him in every way they could. They sent him money and got new members for the Party of the People.

LOST BATTLES

From that year of 1896, Sun Yat-sen traveled around the world. He told people in many countries about the needs of China. He raised money and got his group ready to revolt.

Over and over again he went into China dressed as a Japanese businessman. This was a great risk. For the

Manchus had offered a large sum of money to anybody who would give him up to the police. But no one did. In secret he told members of his party what to do.

During this time the Manchus made the country too weak to defend itself. China lost two wars and had to give up land and money. Ashamed of this, more and more Chinese said a better government was needed. Businessmen wanted railroads and factories. Young men wanted schools. They believed with Sun that once a revolt made a good start, millions of Chinese would help overthrow the Manchus.

In 1900, Sun Yat-sen led his group to battle. But spies had warned the old Empress. Her troops were ready and soon won the battle. The rebels had to flee. Sun escaped this time without much trouble. But the next time he fought the Manchu troops and lost, he was nearly captured. He and his captain put on women's clothes and headdresses which hid their faces like sunbonnets. A boatman carried the two "ladies" to a ship, and they sailed away to safety.

Another time Sun surprised friends in Japan by coming to their home one night. "We heard that you lost the battle!" they cried. "How did you escape? How did you get here?"

"We did lose," he sighed. Then he began to laugh. "But my general and I hid during the night after the

battle. The next day we met two beggars and paid them to change clothes with us. We rubbed dirt on our faces, pinned false queues under our caps, and acted like beggars all the way to the coast. There we took a ship for Japan."

THE BIG REVOLT

In Japan, India, Hawaii, and London, Sun Yat-sen raised money for new revolts. The Party of the People grew larger all the time. From far away he heard of many changes in China. The power of the Empress had grown weaker. She had been forced to let people from other countries build a few railroads. She had

had to start schools. Newspapers were now being printed. All this helped the rebels. At last, China was waking up.

In London a leader of the People's Party said to Dr. Sun, "Nowadays even faraway villagers hear about our work. Those who cannot read gather in tea houses to listen while someone reads newspapers and letters. And the secret societies are growing larger in the cities."

In the year 1911, the big revolt started. People in one southern state after another rose up against the government. Police and troops could not stop them. All the Manchus could do was to keep so many troops near Peking that the rebels did not dare march against the capital.

Sun Yat-sen was traveling far away when he heard what was happening. As fast as he could he hurried to China. At Hong Kong a crowd awaited him, and loud cheers filled the air, "Welcome, Sun Yat-sen! Welcome to free China!"

Already leaders in the People's Party in the South were trying to start a new government. The old Empress was dead, and the boy-Emperor had given up his throne. But Manchu leaders held their power in Peking and the North. The Republic would have to be started in the South, and for a while China would have to be divided.

After a time Sun Yat-sen went north to a city on the coast halfway to Peking. There the Party of the People was meeting. A large crowd came to the house where Sun was staying. As he greeted them they shouted, "You are president of the Republic of China!"

What a triumph! The man who had worked so long for China's freedom thought that his dream was coming true. He began at once to make plans for starting a republic.

But many of the people were too ignorant to understand the change. They did not know what laws to obey. Older people hated the new ways. Northern Chinese did not wish to join any government which had been started by the people of the South.

Hardly two weeks had gone by before another man was pushed forward to be president. He had held a high place in the Manchu government.

Said he, "I have power at the court of Peking and could make the Manchus leave in peace. I am trusted in the North, and I know how to get things done. If I become president and Sun Yat-sen serves under me, we can unite all our people."

Most members of the Party of the People wanted Sun Yat-sen as president. His son begged him to hold his post. But Sun decided to resign.

"If this man can get the Manchus out of Peking and can make all the people in the North and South join in a republic, he should be president. We must do whatever is best for China."

CHINA'S FIRST PRESIDENT

At first all went well. But before a year was up China was again in trouble. People did not trust one another and began to quarrel among themselves. Many of them began to turn against Sun Yat-sen. Battles followed, and at last Sun had to flee for his life to Japan. The president was too selfish to care what happened.

In 1916 the man who headed China's government declared himself emperor. At once an uproar arose in China. The people did not want an emperor, and they refused to obey the ruler's commands. Soon after this the man died. When Sun, who was still in Japan, heard this news he hurried home.

For five more years China was torn by battles and hatreds. At last the southern states decided to set up a government of their own. In 1921, at a great meeting, Sun Yat-sen was chosen to be its president. So, for a time, there were two capitals, one at Peking and one at Canton where Dr. Sun lived. Sad as he was that China was so divided, he hopefully set to work on a new plan of government.

At last in 1924, a meeting of leaders from all over China was held. Then Sun Yat-sen explained his plan. Everyone liked it and voted to accept it.

For weeks after the meeting Dr. Sun went to many cities and towns to tell the people about their new government. Crowds came to hear the famous leader.

Then one day when Dr. Sun came home from one of his long trips, his wife looked at him anxiously. "You are not only tired, you are ill," she said. "You must see a doctor at once."

He sank into a chair. "Yes," he said, "I have known for some time that I am ill. My work for China is over."

Sun Yat-sen did not know how much he had done for his country. No matter what battles and struggles the Chinese go through, to millions of people his very name still means freedom.

Talking Together

1. Why did most Chinese know so little about the people in different parts of their big country?

2. Why did Sun Yat-sen travel so much in China and all over the world?

3. Do you understand what is meant by a revolt? Discuss it in class until every one has a clear idea of exactly what a revolt is.

4. What other things do you know about China besides what is told in this story?

Working Together

1. Plan a dramatization to be called "Scenes from the Life of a Chinese Hero." Decide first what scenes you would like to dramatize and list them. Have only two or three people in each scene, and let them work out just what they are going to do.

2. In the section, "Attack on the Old Gods," the following words and expressions tell the *time* when something happened. The number after each tells the page where it is used.

    afternoon (245)   few weeks (246)   when (258)
    few minutes later (246)   meanwhile (246)
    now (247)   following morning (248)

    Look them up and read the sentences in which they are used. Now divide the class into committees to find the *time* words and expressions used in the other parts of the story. Write sentences using each of them.

3. What did the Party of the People want that China did not have then? How would each of the things they wanted make China a better place in which to live?

4. Write a complete sentence as the title for each of the twelve pictures in the story. For example, for the picture on page 255 you could write, "Tai-cheong brought good news to his family." Read the twelve sentences. What important ideas in the story of Sun Yat-sen that you should remember are shown in the pictures?

To Do by Yourself

1. In the stories you read, many words are used to describe other words. Here are nine words used to describe nine other words that are found in the first part of this story, "Attack on the Old Gods." What do they mean?

narrow path	*dull* life	*lifted* finger
scattered houses	*ignorant* people	*old* writings
slender figure	*dim* light	*new* life

In the other ten parts of the story, see if you can find at least two words in each part which describe other words. Be ready to tell what they mean.

2. Here are names of places used in the story. On a piece of paper make three lists. In the first put the names of places in China; in the second, names of cities not in China; and in the third, names of other countries. Why will one of the names not be on any of the lists?

Hawaii	Washington	Tientsin	Paris
Canton	Hong Kong	New York	India
United States	London	Japan	Peking
	Pearl River		

9 PEACEFUL WARRIOR

GANDHI, The Mahatma

Introduction. *PEACEFUL WARRIOR*

INDIA is one of the oldest countries in the world. It is as large as the eastern part of the United States from our Atlantic coast to the Mississippi River, and it has twice as many people as live in our entire country.

Most of India is very hot and dry. Farmers have a hard time to raise enough grain and cotton. For years there was never enough food for all the millions of people.

Many different groups settled India in the old days. At first they lived in peace and believed in one great religion. Then from other countries came invaders. They divided India in two ways. First, small states ruled by princes were formed. Also, many different religions were brought in.

All the people of India have dark skin, eyes, and hair. But they speak many different languages and have many different customs and beliefs. The Hindus, who were the first settlers, form the largest religious group. Next in size is the Mohammedan group.

In the past Mohammedans thought they must fight those who did not believe as they did. Indian princes often fought with one another, too. Most of the people were kept poor and ignorant because their leaders thought of nothing but war and conquest.

Almost 200 years ago British traders began going to India. British soldiers followed the traders and conquered one

prince after another. Finally the British Government ruled
the whole country. The governor who was sent to rule the
colony was called the Viceroy.

Under British rule wars were put down by soldiers.
Then schools, hospitals, and good roads were built. Young
Indians were taught to be government workers, soldiers,
and policemen. All the people had to obey British laws and
pay heavy taxes. Indians were allowed to elect a National
Congress, but the members could not pass laws.

As more and more young Indians were educated, they began to hate British rule. "We Indians should govern ourselves!" they said.

Yet, in their hearts, they knew this would be a hard task. Most of the people were too ignorant to care who ruled them. They were divided by great differences in religion. Since they did not speak the same language, they did not understand one another. Imagine how hard it would be for the President and Congress of the United States to govern this country if the people in the South and West, the East and North all spoke different languages!

Yet thoughtful Indians were sure that someday they could have their own government. They said to one another, "What we need most is a leader, a 'Mahatma'—a Great Soul —like the ones of ancient times." Finally their wish was granted.

GANDHI

The Mahatma

YOUNG MOHANDAS

IT was just past noon and time for school to be out. The teacher closed his book and looked around at his class of forty boys. They were all dressed in full, white, knee-length trousers and short tunics. The white clothes made their eyes and straight hair and skin look very dark.

Politely the boys waited for the teacher to speak. One of them, however, sat on the edge of his seat ready to spring from the room. The teacher spoke to him.

"Mohandas Gandhi," said the teacher, "do not forget the gymnasium class this afternoon. Everyone must come."

After class most of the pupils walked slowly down the hall, laughing and talking. But Mohandas spoke to nobody. He hurried out of the building. The moment he reached the street he began to run. In spite of the fierce, hot sun he ran without stopping. Finally, he reached a big house set back among palm and banana trees. Pushing open the heavy front door, the boy entered the cool, dark hall. Up the stairs he bounded. In the open doorway of a bedroom he stopped, panting.

There on a white cot a man moved restlessly. "Is that you, Mohandas?" he asked.

"Yes, father." The boy stepped into the darkened room and said anxiously, "Do you feel worse, father? Do you wish a drink of water? What may I do for you?"

A happy smile lighted the face of the sick man. "Read to me, my son. Read some verses from the old, wise teachers."

From the other side of the cot a girl in a white robe rose from her seat. "Mohandas," said she in a timid voice, "will you not eat first? Your mother has food ready for you."

His father spoke quickly. "Yes, go and eat what your mother has ready, my son. Go with your wife and then come back and read."

In silence the boy turned to the door. He waved his hand commandingly to the girl, and she followed him meekly down the stairs.

These two children of fourteen years had been married for a year. Their parents had arranged for the

marriage, but until their wedding day the two had never seen each other. On that day there was an exciting party.

Luckily for Mohandas, his little bride was pretty and sweet. As usual in India, she went home with him to live in his parents' house. They had so much fun together that for a while Mohandas fell behind in school. But now he was hard at work again. He took time from lessons only to help nurse his father.

Mohandas did not get to the gymnasium class on time that afternoon. Next day, when he came back from school, his round face was so sad that his little wife cried out, "What has happened?"

"Hush!" he answered. "I do not want to worry my parents. But I'll tell you that the teacher fined me for missing the gymnasium class."

"Is it much money?" asked the girl anxiously. "I have a little I could give you."

Mohandas shook his head. "I can pay it easily. What troubles me is that the teacher did not believe me when I said I had not judged the time right. He thought I had forgotten and was lying. That shames me. I have never told a lie in my life."

His wife said, "All boys are not like you. Some do lie to escape punishment. But do not grieve, dear. The truth will be known in time."

Mohandas looked happier. "Yes, truth always wins at last."

And so it did. The teacher finally believed the boy and crossed out the fine.

THE SECRET MEAL

Mohandas was not always a good boy. But when he did wrong he never pretended that he was right. Once he deceived his parents. They had brought him up to eat no meat. The Hindus in their group were sure that eating meat made it hard to think about God. Besides, Hindus believe it is wrong to kill animals. Mohandas, however, had a friend who ate meat.

"Because we don't eat meat," said this boy, "we people of India are weak. The English eat meat and are strong. They rule us. We will never drive them out of India unless we also eat meat."

282

Mohandas thought about his friend's idea. He was sure that educated boys should serve their country. Would they grow wiser and stronger by eating meat? Finally, he began eating it in secret. He did not like the taste of it, however, and he hated deceiving his parents.

Often he came back from eating the secret meal to find his mother ready to serve dinner. "Why can't you eat, my son?" she would ask gently.

He would reply that he was not hungry. His girl-wife often said to him, "You are changed since you have this friend. I beg you to give him up."

Mohandas would answer angrily. Yet before the year was over he did give up his friend and also meat eating. He never told his family he had gone against their teaching. But other wrong deeds he confessed and was heartbroken to see his father's grief.

EDUCATION IN ENGLAND

After Mohandas graduated from school, he was sent to England to study law. By this time his father had died. At first his mother was afraid to have him go so far from home and from his Hindu group. But he said to her, "I promise that in England I will never eat meat or drink wine, and I will love my wife faithfully." He could not take his wife to London with him. She now had their baby son to care for.

Living in England was exciting to Mohandas. He tried to do everything in the English way. He wore suits and shirts with stiff collars. He copied English manners and even took dancing lessons. But he made only a few friends among the English people. Many of them made him feel that he belonged to a dark-skinned, conquered race. However, he had friends among the Indian students in London.

Mohandas studied hard and passed the examinations in law. Moreover, he read in English both the Bible and the greatest Indian religious poem. From that time on he was interested in all the religions of the world.

THE YOUNG LAWYER

At the end of three years Mohandas went back to India. He was happy to be with his wife and little son again. At once he started to find work as a lawyer. It took him a long time, however, to earn enough money to support his wife and little boy and a new baby.

Then an Indian merchant asked Mohandas to go to South Africa. He wanted the young lawyer to help win a case between himself and another merchant. Sad as Mohandas was to leave his family, he felt this was a fine chance for work. After a long voyage he landed at the town of Durban on the southeast coast of Africa.

Mohandas Gandhi was just twenty-four years old. Short and thin, with a round, boyish face, he seemed very young. He wore English clothes, but instead of a hat he wound a scarf around his head. This is called a turban and is worn by many men in the Far East.

The rich company employing him was owned by Indians of the Mohammedan religion. They sent one of their men to meet Mohandas at Durban.

"I suppose you know," said the man, "that here in South Africa England has all the power. Both Dutch and English settlers have the right to vote. But the many Negroes and the Indians who live here cannot vote. White men do not treat them as equals."

Mohandas said sadly, "That is true in India, also. But I know many Englishmen who are fair, and I hope to find such men in Pretoria."

Pretoria was the capital of the republic of South Africa, and Gandhi was to work there. He soon set off on his long journey.

It was night when he reached the city. He asked the man at the ticket office where he could get a room. Just then a voice said in his ear, "I think I can help you, mister."

A tall Negro stood by him. "I am an American," he said politely. "I'll take you to a hotel I know."

This he did. The hotel manager said, "I have no feeling against colored people, Mr. Gandhi, and will gladly give you a room. If my white guests do not like to have you in the dining room, I'll send your dinner to your bedroom."

With a sigh Mohandas said that was all right. But soon the manager came to bring him down to dinner. None of the guests had refused to have him sit in the dining room.

The next day the English lawyer with whom Gandhi had to work greeted him warmly. He found the newcomer a boarding place where vegetable meals were served. The Englishman took Mohandas to his church and told him about the Christian religion.

As soon as he was settled, Gandhi invited all the Indians in Pretoria to a meeting. He talked to them about the need of honesty in business and begged them to be clean in every way and to take proper care of garbage and waste. The Indians liked his interest in them and asked for regular meetings. After that Gandhi talked to them often.

At last Gandhi settled the case between the two merchants without going to court. The case was decided in favor of his employer. But Gandhi persuaded the winner to be kind and let the loser pay the debt little by little so that he would not be ruined. In this way both merchants were satisfied, and Gandhi won much honor.

THE INDIAN LEADER

Gandhi's work as a lawyer took him to many cities in the South African Republic. He also traveled in the British state of Natal where the big gold mines were.

Soon he was earning more money than most English lawyers in South Africa. But he would never help a man win a case just to earn money. He had to believe he was in the right.

Once in a court trial Mohandas found that the man who had employed him was lying. Jumping to his feet, Gandhi said to the judge, "Your Honor, I move this case be dismissed without further argument."

The judge praised the young lawyer for his honesty, and the man who had hired him begged his pardon for asking him to take a dishonest case.

As he traveled here and there Gandhi grew sadder about the treatment of Indians. Men who worked in the mines or on farms or as servants were almost slaves. They were forced to work for at least five years with little freedom for themselves. Now a heavy tax was put on these poor people. They were told that those who could not pay it by a certain time would be sent back to India. This was very hard on married men who had families and homes.

In the year 1896, Gandhi returned to India to get help in fighting this law. He wrote a small book about the unjust treatment of Indians in South Africa. Thousands of copies were sold. Newspapers printed stories about it which went to England and South Africa. Gandhi spoke to great crowds in many cities, and Indian leaders promised their help.

Then he returned to South Africa. With his wife and children he sailed for Natal. Many of the English there hated Gandhi because he was the leader of the Indians in South Africa. When he went on shore a mob of men and boys threw stones at him, knocked off his turban, and shouted, "We'll kill you!"

All at once a woman rushed up to him. She was the wife of the chief of police and had always been Gandhi's friend. "Take my arm!" she commanded. "Walk under my umbrella! They will not dare to stone me."

In that way he escaped from the crowd. Later the mob came to the house where he was staying. "Give us Gandhi or we'll tear down the house!" they yelled.

The chief of police, however, quieted the mob. The next day newspapermen wrote that the attack on

Gandhi was wicked. Soon the British Government in London telegraphed that the Natal Government should punish the men who had very nearly killed Gandhi.

"No," said Gandhi to the government men. "Let us forget all the trouble. I only want to do my work."

To the Indians he was a hero. They came in crowds to his meetings. Gandhi's wife was proud of him. She was eager to help him.

"Whatever we do," Mohandas said to her, "must be done in a peaceful way. I have been reading some wonderful books about how wrong all violence is. A brave man will die for his beliefs, but he will not harm others."

A GOOD EXAMPLE

Gandhi felt that both the English and the rich Indian merchants must be told how bad things were for poor and helpless Indians. Therefore he helped start a weekly paper called *Indian Opinion*. In this paper he asked for help in getting the government to do away with laws unfair to Indians. But at the same time he wrote, "A man should work for his rights, but he must never hurt or hate his enemies. To be worthy of God's help a man must live a good life."

He himself set the example. He spent his fortune in helping others. He lived like the poorest man, caring nothing for clothes or comforts. He ate only fruit, vegetables, and nuts. He attacked wrong things that his fellow Indians did.

In his paper he wrote that one of the chief Hindu teachings was bad. Hindus had been taught that they were born into certain groups and that there they stayed. To belong to the top group people had to be born into it. They could not rise to it by hard work or noble deeds. Below the highborn people were other groups. The people in the lowest group were called "Untouchables." To touch such a person or drink from the same well was thought poisonous. Gandhi had never believed that people were divided this way at birth.

One day at a gold mine in Natal he watched the miners come out from work. Armed guards stood all around to keep order. Gandhi saw a young boy come out of the dark mine blinking at the sunlight. All at once the boy darted past a guard. He sprang up on a bank of earth and picked a great white flower growing there. His thin, dark face bent over the flower lovingly.

Because the boy had gone out of bounds, the guard started for him. But Gandhi reached him first. From the way the boy was dressed, it was plain to see that he was an Untouchable. Yet Gandhi's arms went around the thin body.

"Have no fear, my little brother," he said softly. "I will protect you. You love flowers as I do. You are no outcast. We are the same."

Looking up at the guard, Gandhi said in English, "And you are my brother, too, even though you do hateful work here. Leave this boy alone. He has done no harm."

As he watched the boy run off Gandhi felt his heart almost burst with pity. "There must come an end to all these divisions among Hindus," he cried.

VICTORY WITHOUT FIGHTING

From then on Gandhi worked against these divisions among Hindus. He broke the Hindu rules on purpose. In his law office he hired young people born as Untouchables. He brought them to his home for meals. At first his wife was shocked, but she came to see that these were acts of love. Gandhi wrote in the *Indian Opinion* that Hindus must give up these old, wrong ideas. Then he made plans to prove that the different groups of Hindus could live and work together.

In 1904 he started a colony near Durban on a large farm. Many of his followers built huts there and raised their own vegetables and fruit. Of course Mrs. Gandhi and the children lived there, and Mohandas was with them except when traveling on law cases. He loved singing with all the children on the farm and taking them on walks. He played jokes on them and laughed with them. In this colony children learned how to settle their quarrels without fighting.

About this time the English passed a law forcing every Indian in South Africa to be fingerprinted in police courts. If the Dutch and the English had been made to do the same thing, the law would have been fair. But it was meant to mark the Indians as people who might become criminals. The Indians held a great meeting of protest. But few of the speakers knew what to tell the people to do.

At last Gandhi got up to speak. He looked small and young as he faced the huge audience. Instead of shouting as the other speakers had, he spoke softly. "This law was passed to stamp us as people lower than white men. It is not fair, and I do not mean to obey it. I will not be fingerprinted. I should rather go to jail."

Everyone gasped. But he went on, "If I disobey a law I shall be arrested, perhaps beaten and starved. I may be fined and lose all my property. But I should rather have that happen than give in to this law."

From all parts of the hall people shouted, "We too will disobey the law! We will go to jail also!"

Gandhi held up his thin hand. "Remember, however, that such action will do no good unless it is done peacefully. You must never resist the police or do one violent act."

After that Gandhi led his followers to protest also the law taxing the poor miners. For the first time women helped by getting people to join the protest. They even went to the mines and were arrested for talking to the workers. Almost at once the workers went on a strike. Then the mine owners cut off lights, food, and water from the strikers.

As days went by, the strikers became hungry and angry. Gandhi was afraid that they would do some violence. As he hurried to Natal, he decided that it would be better if they were sent to prison where they would be fed and housed.

At Natal he talked to hundreds of miners. "We must show the government in a gentle way that Indians will no longer stand unjust treatment. Are you and your families willing to go to jail without striking one blow against the police?"

With one voice the men said they were willing. Then Gandhi told the miners his plan. "There is an old rule that says no one can cross the borders between the South African states without permission. We will break that rule. We will march peacefully across the border of Natal!"

Five thousand men with their families started on the march. Gandhi begged food for them from rich Indian

merchants. He and his helpers showed the others how to make camp each night. Over the hot plains and down the rough valley-trails the great crowd marched. At night they sang old hymns and prayed.

Gandhi's plan worked. At the border, policemen arrested the marchers and sent them back to the mines. As prisoners they had to be fed and housed. Gandhi and other leaders were put in jail. No one resisted. Their peaceful protest won sympathy everywhere.

In other South African states workers followed the example and went on strike. Jails were crowded. People in England and India heard about what was happening and became much excited. Many men said the government must listen to the peaceful protests. Even the Viceroy of India sent word to London that justice must be done.

Finally the government leaders listened to the protests coming from white men and Indians alike. Then all prisoners were set free. The tax on the workers was taken off and so was the rule that they must work for five years like slaves. The fingerprinting law was also blotted out. There was great rejoicing among Indians everywhere. The wonderful thing was that the great victory had been won without fighting or violence.

THE NEW COLONY

When at last Gandhi returned to India, the ship landed at Bombay. As the small, dark man in his white robe came down the gangplank cries of joy went up from shore. A huge crowd of Indians had come to meet him.

That evening at a friend's house he asked, "How is it possible that there are so many people who seem to know me?"

His friend laughed. "Your great victory in South Africa has made you famous. Because you won it without violence or hate, our hearts are moved. You have shown us that love and self-sacrifice are more powerful than guns."

For a year Gandhi traveled over the country to learn how the people of India lived. He met most of the religious leaders and teachers and those who were working for India's freedom in the National Congress.

His next step was to start a little colony in the western part of India. Its first members were Mrs. Gandhi and the children and some of the families who had helped him in South Africa. Soon many students and teachers gathered there. They shared all the work.

Before long Gandhi took into his colony a family of Untouchables. All the other members welcomed them. But Hindus outside the colony were shocked. A neighbor who used the same well as the colonists was angry. He thought that because the Untouchables dipped their pitchers in the well, the water was not fit to drink. Many of the rich Hindus who had given money to start the colony would send no more help. Then came a day when there was no money for food. Gandhi did not know what to do.

Then one morning a big motor car drove into the village. Out of it stepped a Mohammedan. He said to Gandhi, "I should like to help this group. Will you take help from me even though I am not a Hindu?"

"Most certainly," smiled Mohandas. "We shall be grateful for any help you wish to give us."

Next day the Mohammedan came back and handed Gandhi a bag filled with money—enough to last the villagers a whole year.

TWO BIG PLANS

Gandhi found out that thousands of workers in India were treated just as Indians had been treated in South Africa. They were forced to work for five years at the same low wage. If a man left his job, he could be brought back by force. So Gandhi wrote articles for newspapers and made speeches telling people how the workers were treated. Everyone in India became stirred, and the government had to act.

In time this unfair way of treating workers was stopped. No wonder that millions of Indians began to look upon Gandhi as their great leader. No wonder, either, that the English began to fear his power.

Gandhi worked with the National Congress in demanding that the British give Indians a share in making laws. The government promised that it would do this some day, but did not keep the promise. Instead, all of the soldiers were told to keep peace by force. Then when riots started, the soldiers shot the rioters down.

Over and over again Gandhi kept his people from revolting. "Let us not try to take revenge for wrong acts," he said. "Let us work in a peaceful way."

Whatever else he was doing, Gandhi kept two big plans moving along. One was to get Mohammedans and Hindus to drop their quarrels and to work together for Indian freedom.

His other plan was to get Indians to make more things for themselves instead of buying so much from English merchants. He decided that the first step was to teach country people and villagers to spin and weave. If they learned to make cotton cloth for their robes, they would not have to buy English cloth.

A rich Indian lady found a few spinning wheels and looms. She also found some women who knew how to spin and weave. They taught their skill to members of Gandhi's colony. In turn, the members taught others.

Before long thousands of villagers all over India were making cotton cloth. This made it possible for many people to stop buying expensive English cottons. Homespun clothes became the uniform of rich and poor, of everyone devoted to Indian freedom.

The men in Congress believed that Indians could do still more. They decided that no products should

300

be brought into the country from England. This meant that people would have to do without many things they wanted. But to Gandhi's joy, people all over the land were ready to make sacrifices for India.

Something else made him even happier. The Hindu members of the Congress agreed that no longer must there be any Untouchable group. By loving acts Gandhi had persuaded the leaders to overthrow a belief that had been held by Hindus for 3000 years.

THE MAHATMA

The people of India now began to speak of Gandhi as the "Mahatma," which means "Great Soul." For years he had taught Indians how to resist the British without hate or violence. The British knew that often it was Gandhi alone who kept millions of down-trodden people from violence against their rulers.

Once an Indian mob killed a number of policemen. Gandhi, taking all the blame upon himself as the leader, went on a fast. For nearly a month he would not eat a bite of food. Fear that he might die frightened the rioters, and they promised to be quiet and patient.

Because, however, Gandhi kept right on leading people to disobey laws which he thought were unfair, the government finally arrested him.

At his trial Gandhi said to the judge, "I am guilty, and it is your duty to punish me. But my duty as an

Indian citizen is to work against a government which has done so much harm to my country."

Gently the judge replied, "Most people in India will be sorry that my government cannot let you go free. But laws must be obeyed."

In his prison cell Gandhi read, studied, and wrote letters to people all over the world. His jailers were as worried as his followers when he became very ill. So was the government. If the Mahatma died in jail, the people might rise up against those who put him there. The Viceroy ordered that the prisoner be sent home.

In the year 1924, Gandhi persuaded the Indian Congress to elect Jawaharlal Nehru to help run it. Nehru was handsome, well educated, and a hard worker for India's freedom. Gandhi knew he would be a good leader.

Nehru loved Gandhi almost as much as he did his own father. He called him "Bapu," which means "father." But he thought "Bapu" was too patient. He said to him, "You and my father want India to be like Canada—to have self-government as part of the British Empire. Why shouldn't we be a separate country?"

The two men were seated on straw mats on the floor of Gandhi's little hut. Gandhi leaned over and patted Nehru's knee. "My dear young friend," said he, "you don't seem to know that there are not enough of us yet who will make sacrifices for freedom."

Then he went on to explain. "Mohammedans will not yet work with Hindus. Yet they must if we are to have a government for India. Many Indians who have government jobs would hate to lose them. Don't you see? Few people are ready for change. However, I am willing to do as the Congress says."

The struggle between Congress and the British Government went right on. But the British would not yield. Then a campaign of disobedience began all over the country. People did not pay taxes. Workers went on strike.

Gandhi led a huge crowd of people on a long march to protest against the tax on salt. He took them to the sea to get salt. This was really play-acting, for he

could not hope to get much salt that way. But people knew it was a way of fighting the British, and at every village they came with flowers and food to cheer the marchers on their way. They called him "Mahatma" and knelt at his feet.

Again Gandhi was arrested. But his arrest could not stop the disobedience of the people. In a few months thousands of Hindus and Mohammedans were in prison. The British Government did not know what to do. But hundreds of Englishmen said that the Indians must be allowed to govern themselves.

TOWARD FREEDOM

At last, in January, 1931, the Viceroy sent for Gandhi. Sitting in his chair in the most beautiful room of the palace, the Viceroy looked like the most powerful governor in the world, which he was. But sitting beside him was a small, white-robed, bare-legged man with sandals on his feet. This man was even more powerful.

"My friend," said the Viceroy, "are you satisfied with this plan? All prisoners will be freed. The tax on salt will be taken off. The Indian Congress will be asked to help us make a new constitution which will give India self-government under British rule. This will be a great step."

Gandhi accepted the plan. That year he went to London. He went to talk with men in the government about the new Constitution.

As he walked along the streets children followed him. They made fun of this bare-legged man in a white robe. And at first they laughed and jeered at him. But Gandhi was so friendly that soon the children were calling him "Uncle Gandhi."

That trip was disappointing, for England did not want to give up ruling India. When Nehru and Gandhi fought against delay, they were put in jail.

When he was once more free, Gandhi returned to his village. People from all over the world came to see him. They wanted to hear him talk about religion, about life, and about India. Everyone enjoyed his gay laughter and his wisdom.

In the year 1937, the new government of India was started. England kept soldiers in the country and had the final say about important things. But now elections were held and the people took a real part in their own government. Gandhi rejoiced that at last his people were learning to rule themselves. But Nehru was not satisfied.

"Bapu," he exclaimed, "we can stand on our own feet now! Why don't the British leave us alone?"

When World War II broke out in 1939 Gandhi believed at first that India should stay out of war. But later he began to agree with Nehru and said, "If we must defend our country, let us have our own generals like free people."

In the summer of 1942, the Indian Congress passed the "Quit India" bill. This meant that every English soldier and government worker must leave the country. Immediately all Indian leaders were arrested.

At the end of the war the British Government granted India complete freedom to govern itself. At last, India was an independent nation. Gandhi, the Mahatma, had led his people to freedom.

For a time the new nation had many troubles. Mohammedans and Hindus began to quarrel. But Gandhi kept saying, "Why should we hate one another? Why should we sink back into darkness when the sun of freedom shines upon us?"

When fighting kept on, he protested by going on a fast. Soon he became very weak. In the house of a friend he lay on a cot and refused to eat or drink. Word was spread that the Mahatma might die. He was too old and frail to stand starvation. All over the world people waited anxiously for news.

At last word of peace was brought to him. Leaders of Mohammedans and Hindus said they would stop fighting and try to work out an agreement. Then Gandhi began to eat a little. Soon he grew stronger.

One January day in 1948, he stepped out of doors for a meeting with his followers. As he walked into the garden, he leaned on the arms of his secretaries. Everyone watched with joy.

At that moment a shot rang out. Gandhi sank down upon the grass. The bullet had struck him.

Some of the people ran to capture the murderer. He was a young student who hated Gandhi's wish to make peace with Mohammedans.

Others ran to the figure on the grass. "I forgive—" murmured Gandhi as he died.

His limp body was carried back to his cot. All night long friends watched beside him in deep grief.

Nehru told the Indian people by radio what had happened. He was so stricken by the loss of his beloved "Bapu" that he could hardly speak.

"Friends and comrades," said he, "the light has gone out of our lives." Then he begged everyone to pray. "The greatest prayer is to pledge ourselves to serve the truth and the cause for which this great countryman of ours lived and for which he has died."

All India was stunned by this loss. Mohammedans joined with Hindus in prayer and mourning. As the news of Gandhi's death spread around the world, messages poured in. Kings and presidents, students and artists, simple folk and famous persons mourned this wonderful man.

Today Indians believe that his spirit watches over the land. They believe the words of Nehru: "Gandhi, our master, still speaks to us. His voice is the voice of truth, and truth can never be put down."

Talking Together

1. Both Livingstone and Gandhi lived in Africa. In what ways was the work they did different? In what ways was it something the same?

2. When Gandhi finally returned to India to live, why did he not continue being a lawyer as he had in South Africa?

3. Show how Gandhi helped the Indian people to get what they wanted without fighting a war.

4. What is meant by *government*? Discuss all the things *government* did in the story of Gandhi. What does *government* do in the United States today?

Working Together

1. Make a booklet with large pages called "Leaders in Other Lands." Divide the class into nine committees. Each committee will plan one page on the hero assigned to it. You should try to make your page as attractive as you can. It should have enough information on it to tell something about your hero to others who do not know as much about him as you do.

2. Take a piece of wrapping paper the length you want and turn it sidewise. On it draw a series of pictures in color telling the story of Mohandas Gandhi. Such a series is called a frieze. Choose your own scenes or use some of these: (a) Gandhi studying a law book in London; (b) Gandhi at the ticket office in Pretoria, South Africa; (c) a crowd meets Gandhi's ship at Bombay; (d) the Mohammedan gives Gandhi money; (e) Gandhi and the Viceroy; (f) Gandhi lying on a cot fasting.

To Do by Yourself

1. The one thing that all the sentences in a *paragraph* tell about is called the *topic* of the *paragraph*. What is the *topic* of each of these *paragraphs?* The *paragraph* on p. 286 beginning "As soon as . . ." The *paragraph* on p. 288 beginning "As he traveled . . ." The *paragraph* on p. 291 beginning "In his paper . . ." The *paragraph* on p. 295 beginning "Five thousand . . ." If you are not sure what the *topic* is, read each sentence by itself and think what each one tells about. Then decide what one thing all of the sentences tell about. That one thing is called the *topic*.

2. Make a sentence for a "Guess Who" game. Make believe you are an important person in one of the stories of the book. Begin your sentence, "I . . ." and then tell something that important person did. See if your classmates can guess who you are.

3. Here are some events, or happenings, in the life of Gandhi but not in the order in which they happened. Copy on a piece of paper the event that happened first, then the one that came second, and so on until you have all six events in the right order.

   Nehru worked with Gandhi
   Went to England to study law
   Started a paper called *Indian Opinion*
   World War II
   Indians were taught to spin and weave
   Worked in South Africa

Index

Africa, exploration and
settlement, 134–135; *map*,
133. *See also* Livingstone,
David *and* South Africa

Air routes, 170

Alps (ălps) Mountains, 88

Altarpiece (ôl'tēr-pēs),
Leonardo's, of Madonna
with Christ Child and
St. Anne, 99

Amundsen, Roald
(ä'mo͞on-sĕn, rō'äl), 202

Apprentice (à-prĕn'tĭs), 42, 46,
47

Arabs, 135, 151, 160–163;
illus., 161, 164–165

Arctic Ocean, 171, 192

Arno (är'nō) River, 81, 83

Atlantic Ocean, 137, 152, 154,
155

Atoms, 226

Bergen (bĕr'gĕn), Norway, 181

Bering (bēr'ĭng) Strait, 188
map, 172

Bible, 40, 41, 51, 284;
Gutenberg's, 65–66, 68;
Gandhi reads, 284

Birmingham (bûr'mĭng-ăm),
England, 122, 123, 126, 130

Boers (bōrz), 135, 141, 143, 150

Bombay (bŏm-bā'), 297

Books: hand-copied, 40–42, 52;
illus., 41, 52; spread of,
through printing, 68–69.
See also Gutenberg, Johann
and Printing

Boulton, Matthew
(bōl'tŭn, măth'ū), 122–127,
130; *illus.*, 125

Bronya (brôn'yà), sister of
Marie Curie, 210–211, 212,
217, 219–220, 222, 227

Canals, 122, 123

Cantlie (kănt'lĭ), Dr., 254, 255, 263–266

Canton (kăn-tŏn'), China, 249–251, 253, 257, 260, 272; *illus.*, 241

Cape Town, South Africa, 135, 138, 140, 153; *illus.*, 140

Charles VII, King of France: as prince, 3, 7–8, 10, 12, 13–14; receives Jeanne d'Arc, 17–19; *illus.*, 18; crowned at Reims, 27–28; a weak king, 28–30; drives English from France, 36

China, *map*, 277; free spirit of, 242–244. *See also* Sun Yat-sen

Chinon (shē-nôn'), France, 10, 12, 17–19; *illus.*, 20–21

Christ Child: Leonardo's sketch of, 85–87; Leonardo's altarpiece of, with Madonna and St. Anne, 99. *See also* Jesus

Christian (krĭs'chăn) Mission of the Church of England, Canton, China, 250

Christianity (krĭs-chĭ-ăn'ĭ-tĭ), 40–41, 135, 242, 247

Chuma (chōō'må), Livingstone's helper, 162, 163, 166

Clermont (klâr'mŏnt), Robert Fulton's steamboat, 129

Clyde (klīd) River, 111, 115; *illus.*, 111

Coal mines, 110, 117, 121; *illus.*, 125

Cobbler, 108; *illus.*, 216

Congo (kŏng'gō) River, 135

Copyists, 42

Curie, Eve (kū'rē', ēv), daughter of Marie and Pierre, 230, 231, 237, 238

Curie, Irene, daughter of Marie and Pierre, 217, 229, 231, 238

Curie, Marie: arrives in Paris from Warsaw, 209–211; *illus.*, 209; studies at the University of Paris, 211–212; meets and marries Pierre, 212–215; *illus.*, 213, 214; interest in X ray, 215–217; *illus.*, 216; experiments with uranium, 218–221; *illus.*, 219; discovers polonium, 222; discovers radium, 221–227; *illus.*, 205, 223, 225; receives degree from the University of Paris, 227–228; receives Nobel prize, 228–230; *illus.*, 229, 231; teaches at the University of Paris, 232; work in First World War, 232–236; *illus.*, 235; receives gift of radium from United States, 236–237; a great woman, 237–238

316

Monastery (mŏn'ăs-tĕr-ĭ), 40, 53, 84, 87
Monks (mŭngks), 40, 41, 52, 53, 84, 87; *illus.*, 41

Nansen, Eva Sars (nän'sĕn, ēvá särs), wife of Fridtjof, 181–182, 187, 189, 199; *illus.*, 182
Nansen, Fridtjof (frēt'yŏf): described, 171, 182; joins sealing ship, 173–181; *illus.*, 177, 178, 180; love of Far North, 181–182; crosses Greenland, 182–187; *illus.*, 169, 182, 186; plans trip to North Pole, 187–189; icebound in Arctic Ocean, 189–192; attempts dash to Pole, 192–195; *illus.*, 193; winters in Franz Josef Land, 194–198; *illus.*, 196; returns as hero to Norway, 198–202; *illus.*, 200–201; *map* of explorations, 172
Natal (nä-täl'), 287, 289–290, 291, 295
Negroes, enslavement of, in South Africa, 135, 140–141, 150, 151, 160–162; Livingstone's relations with, 141–142, 144, 159; *illus.*, 145, 146, 148–149, 160, 161, 164–165

Nehru, Jawaharlal (nä-rōō', jä-wä'hár-läl), 302–303, 305–306, 308
Newcomen (nū-kŭm'ĕn), Thomas, 110, 117, 118, 123
New Testament, 51
New York Herald, 164, 166
Niger (nī'jĕr) River, 135
Nobel (nō-bĕl'), Alfred, 228
Nobel prize, 228–229
Norsemen, 170
North. *See* Far North
North Pole, 171; Nansen's expedition to, 187–195
Northern lights, 174
Norway, 171

Ocean currents. *See* Sea currents
Oluf (ō'lŏŏf), Nansen's weatherman, 185
Orleans (ôr-lä-än'), France, 2, 13, 19; French victory at, 22–25
Orleans, Duke of, 2
Oslo (ôs'lōō), capital of Norway, 176, 181, 184, 187, 199; harbor, *illus.*, 200–201
Otto, Nansen's captain, 185, 186, 189, 192, 193, 199

Paris, capital of France, 2, 103, 209–211; Jeanne d'Arc leads army against, 28–29
Paris, University of, 210, 227, 230, 232

318

Watt (wŏt), James: childhood,
III–114; *illus.*, 107, 112–113;
described, 112, 114, 126;
learns about tool-making in
London, 114–116; *illus.*, 116;
opens shop in Glasgow, 116–
117, 120; experiments with
steam engine, 117–122; *illus.*,
119; works on canals, 122,
123; perfects steam engine,
122–127; *illus.*, 125; settles
in Birmingham, 123, 126,
130; one of world's great
inventors, 127–130; his last
years, 130
Watt, Mr., father of James,
III, 113–114, 115, 116;
illus., 107
Watt, Peggy, wife of James,
117, 119, 120, 121, 123

Weavers, 42, 44
Weaving, machines for, 109,
129; encouraged by Gandhi
in India, 300
Westminster Abbey
(wĕst'mĭn-stēr ăb'ĭ), 130,
166
Whales, 177, 181
Wise Men, Leonardo's sketch
of, 85–87
Wood-block, 50, 53
Wood carver, 49
Wood-print, 51

X ray, 215–217; in First World
War, 234–235

Zambesi (zăm-bā'zē) River,
151, 153, 156–158, 159–160

920
EAT

EATON, Jeanette.
Leaders in other lands.

Date Due			
OCT 2 0 64			
NOV 6 '52			
FEB 2 1 66			
LM			
NOV 18 70			
NOV 3 0 1983			
MAY 6 1988			
DEC 2 4 '96			